4. 4. 80

The Oldest Library Motto

and Other Library Essays

ΨΙΧΗΣ ΙΑΤΡΕΙΟΝ

THE LIBRARY MOTTO IN THE GREAT HALL OF THE LIBRARY AT ST. GALL

Die Stiftsbibliothek Sank Gallen

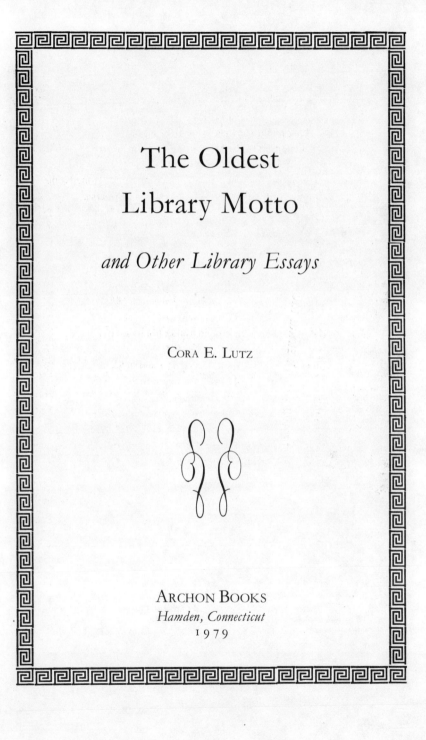

The Oldest Library Motto

and Other Library Essays

Cora E. Lutz

Archon Books

Hamden, Connecticut

1979

© Cora E. Lutz 1979
First published 1979 as an Archon Book,
an imprint of the Shoe String Press Inc,
Hamden, Connecticut 06514
Composed in Garamond by Asco Trade Typesetting Ltd of Hong Kong
Lithoprinted and bound in the United States of America

Library of Congress Cataloging in Publication Data
LUTZ, CORA ELIZABETH
The oldest library motto, and other library essays.

Includes bibliographical references and index.
1. Books—Addresses, essays, lectures.
2. Manuscripts—Addresses, essays, lectures.
3. Libraries—Addresses, essays, lectures.
I. Title.
Z4.L85   001.55'2   79-16757
ISBN 0-208-01816-6

The following essays first appeared in the *Yale University Library Gazette:* "The Letter of Lentulus Describing Christ" (1975); "Le Bon Chien Soullart" (1977); "The 'Gentle Puritan' and the 'Angelic Doctor'" (1978), "A Forged Manuscript in Boustrophedon" (1978), "The Clock of Eternal Wisdom" (1978), and "The American Unicorn" (1979). "The Oldest Library Motto" first appeared in *The Library Quarterly* at the University of Chicago (1978).

To my sister
Hazel P. Lutz

Contents

7

ILLUSTRATIONS

9

Preface

LONG BEFORE AND EVER SINCE Horace Walpole revealed the existence of the Land of Serendip where the three princes "were always making discoveries by accidents or sagacity of things they were not in search of," most habitual frequenters of libraries have found for themselves that wonderful country. My own introduction came when, as a child, in some now-forgotten context, I came upon the magic phrase "the music of the spheres." Thereafter, for some time, I was lulled to sleep every night by that celestial harmony. Since then, in the great libraries of Europe and in this country, I have happened upon unexpected clues, some of which proved to be will-o'-the-wisps that vanished, but more that have led me on pleasant excursions into interesting byways. These essays record some of these detours that were motivated by accidental encounters in libraries.

The title of the book comes from the beautiful library of St. Gall. Some years ago when I was in search of a unique manuscript that contains a drawing of one of the first telescopes, my attention was claimed by an inscription in Greek engraved upon a scroll above the great doors of the main hall of the library—ΨΥΧΗΣ ΙΑΤΡΕΙΟΝ. I translate it "House of Healing for the Soul." Not surprisingly, that splendid phrase kept pursuing me until I decided to search for its original setting. The results are the subject of the first essay.

The subjects of most of the other essays suggested themselves to me, obviously, during the time that I was cataloguing the pre-1600 manuscripts in the Beinecke Library at Yale. They are all based upon literature of the Middle Ages or the Renaissance. The subjects of the other essays came to my attention by more devious routes. The Y of Pythagoras, for example, first became known to me when I was studying the satires of Persius in college, but it made no great impression upon me then. Later, when I was working on the text of a ninth-century commentary on Martianus Capella, Remigius' explanation of the symbol led me to investigate other early references to it. But the whole subject remained dormant in my mind until recently, when I was looking for the printer's device of a Bohemian publisher and happened upon Geoffroy Tory's magnificent printer's device—a glorified Y of Pythagoras.

My interest in Musonius Rufus' quotation of a Roman proverb is also of long standing. When I was editing the Greek text, I sought in vain for clues to the provenance of the saying, but did not look into its later use. My interest was renewed recently when, in seeking references to the existence of the unicorn in America, I went through Hakluyt's accounts of the English navigators and came upon the proverb in Sir Humphrey Gilbert's *Discourse of a Discoverie for a New Passage to Cataia*. This prompted a search for other instances of the use of the saying in the literature of the sixteenth century.

The sympathy Copernicus had for the humanist movement was brought to my notice by way of Byzantine Greek. My introduction to Theophylactus Simocatta's long history of the reign of the emperor Maurice struck me as far less interesting than his preface which is in the form of a dialogue between History and Philosophy. Yet the substance of that, too, escaped my mind and only the euphonious name of the author remained, when, by chance, I came upon it in a different context. In investigating the career of Bishop Dubravius of Bohemia, in a history of literature, I came upon an account of Copernicus' literary activities that included his translation of the Epistles of Simocatta. This led me to a consideration of the whole matter of the beginning of the humanistic movement in Bohemia.

The last three essays differ entirely from the rest in that they are discussions of single books and all relate to the early president of Yale, Ezra Stiles. They are included because they illustrate so precisely the phenomenon of serendipity. I came upon the books, quite unexpectedly, in my own home. When Mrs. Amelia Foote Roe moved to New Zealand some years ago, she asked me to store several boxes of books for her. Later, after I had examined in the Beinecke Library the first medieval manuscript ever to come to Yale and had studied the marginal comments of Ezra Stiles in the volume, I wrote up my conclusions and sent a copy to Mrs. Roe, who is a direct descendant of Ezra Stiles. She replied that possibly I might find something of interest among the books she had left with me. When I opened the boxes, I found a rare treasure of books from the Stiles library. They are part of what was a large collection of Stiles books and papers first assembled by Emilia Stiles Leavitt and added to by five generations of Stiles descendants. Now most of the collection is in the Yale library. From the remaining books, now in my possession, I have chosen to describe three that reflect eighteenth-century attitudes toward three significant aspects of American culture.

In preparing this book, I have enjoyed the privilege of using the great resources of the Sterling Memorial Library and the Beinecke Rare Book and Manuscript Library of Yale University. I should like to take this opportunity to thank their librarians and staffs for the innumerable courtesies they extended to me and for their unfailing assistance in the course of my research.

Many of these essays have been printed in the *Yale University Library Gazette*, and I wish to express my appreciation to the editor, Donald C. Gallup, for granting permission to reprint them here. I should also like to thank E. Boyd Bayward, editor of *The Library Quarterly* of the University of Chicago, for permitting me to reprint one of the essays. I gratefully acknowledge the kindness of the Stiftsbibliothek of St. Gall, the Beinecke Rare Book and Manuscript Library of Yale, Yale University Art Gallery, and the New Haven Colony Historical Society in allowing the reproduction of illustrations from their libraries. For her very great generosity in presenting me with a collection of rare books from the Stiles library, my deepest gratitude goes to Mrs. Amelia Foote Roe.

New Haven   C.E.L.

ΨΥΧΗΣ ΙΑΤΡΕΙΟΝ

The Oldest Library Motto

LATE IN THE SUMMER of 1976, the mummy of Rameses II, which had been sent from the Cairo Museum to the Louvre, was given a welcome to Paris such as is usually accorded to governing heads of state. Like a long-delayed appearance of the hero in a play, the arrival of the mummy immediately galvanized interest in the spectacular exhibition of the art of the reign of the Egyptian Pharaoh, Rameses the Great (1293–1225 B.C.) in the Galéries Nationales du Grand Palais.[1] The splendor of the gold objects, the rich jewelry, the wall-paintings, the great statues and architectural remains were suddenly transferred from the realm of fantasy to the real world as the actual achievements of Rameses II. His incredible military exploits, his personal domination of his age, as well as the vast temples, tombs, and colossal statues that he had caused to be erected were somehow now more comprehensible. Yet there was a grim irony associated with it: all that was left of this man—who had had carved upon his statue words of defiance to the world and posterity to surpass even one

of his mighty works and who had sought eternal life by the most
extraordinary means—was now in Paris to be treated for a
physical disease that was threatening to destroy the pitiful
remains of his person.[2]

For one group of people, the bibliophiles, however, a more
fitting memorial to the mighty Pharaoh than all of the splendid
material treasures and of greater interest than the mummy was
the spiritual legacy left in the form of an inscription placed
above the portals of his library, an inscription which designated
the library as "the house of healing for the soul." We owe the
preservation of the words to Diodorus Siculus,[3] who, writing in
the last century before our era, records them in his Greek *History
of the World* in the section on Egypt, for which he had drawn
chiefly from the work of the third-century historian, Hecataeus
of Abdera. Diodorus outlines at length the accomplishments of
Rameses II, whom he calls "Osymandias," a distortion of the
royal title, "Usima-re." He also describes the great complex of
buildings at Thebes, now known as the Ramesseum, with its
temples, tombs, and royal palace, and speaks in some detail of
the countless statues, unusual paintings, and extensive reliefs. Of
the great hall which housed the library of sacred books, however,
he gives only the Greek translation of the inscription.

The striking phrase might well have been adopted by the
literary Romans, but strangely enough it was not. Apparently
Cicero did not know it, for he seems to have been searching for
those very words. In explaining the release from mental stress
and the psychic restoration that he experienced when he could be
alone with his books, he used the phrases "pabulum animorum"
("food for souls"), "pastus animorum" ("nourishment for the
spirit"), and "medicina animae" ("medicine for the soul").[4]
Even these felicitous phrases seem not to have been widely
quoted and they were never applied to libraries. Indeed,
Rameses' inscription seems to have been used appropriately for
the first time when the Greek words were incised and painted on
a gilded scroll above the doorway of the main hall of the
beautiful baroque library of St. Gall when it was built about

1760, some three thousand years after the original. How it happened that its revival occurred in the remote Alpine library is an interesting story.

In an often-quoted letter, Poggio Bracciolini,[5] the noted Italian humanist and unrivalled book-collector, tells of his experience in seeking and finding manuscripts at St. Gall. While he was attending the Council of Constance in 1414, Poggio took the opportunity to visit the libraries of some of the old Swiss monasteries. The Benedictine house of St. Gall, which had had a remarkable history of religious, cultural, and literary achievements in the ninth and tenth centuries, had suffered a sad decline. With a relaxation of discipline and a consequent loss of interest in scholarship, the once-famous library was utterly neglected. So it was that Poggio discovered there numerous treasures that had long been forgotten, for example, the works of Quintilian and several orations of Cicero. Some of these manuscripts he had copied; others he carried away and they were never returned. Perhaps in a similar book-hunting expedition elsewhere, he came across a manuscript of the *History* of Diodorus Siculus. At any rate, before 1455, Poggio had translated that work into Latin. It was printed in Bologna in 1472 and reprinted in at least five other editions before the end of the fifteenth century, and in six more in the sixteenth century. Then Latin translations by other scholars also began to be printed. In 1539, a Greek edition was printed in Basel, and Stephanus produced the Greek text in Geneva in 1559. By the end of the century, translations into French, German, Italian, and English had appeared. Happily the sixteenth century saw a revival of interest in books and scholarship at the abbey of St. Gall, particularly under the leadership of Abbot Otmar Kunz.[6] It was this cleric who obtained for the library the 1559 Greek edition of Diodorus. Later the 1539 edition and the 1515 edition of Poggio's Latin translation came to the library.

Not only was the text of the *History* available, but it was being read, and the aptness of the inscription over Rameses' library was noted. The great Belgian scholar, Justus Lipsius (1547–1602), for example, in his *De Bibliothecis Syntagma* gives the quotation in Greek, cites his source in Diodorus, and comments on the library of Osymandias.[7] Attention is called to Lipsius' account by Johann Samuel Misander in his *Bücher-Freunde und Bücher-Feinde*, published in 1695, but he gives the important phrase in Latin— "Medicam animae officinam."[8] In Hamburg in 1682, R. Capel's *Lectionum bibliothecariarum memorabilium Syntagma* was published. On the elaborate title page of the book is an engraving[9] depicting the colonnaded entrance to a library, over the archway of which the Greek inscription appears, and on the steps leading to the entrance there is a paraphrase of Virgil—"Procul late profani," and of Horace—"Odi profanum vulgus et arceo, favete pii bonique."[10] One of the most striking instances of the adoption of the motto occurred in Sweden in 1710 when the learned scholar, Eric Benzelius, had the words, translated into Swedish, stamped in gold upon the covers of the vellum-bound books in the library of the Royal University at Upsala.[11]

The present distinguished librarian at St. Gall, Dr. Johannes Duft, in his account of the library has given some interesting details of the background to the building of that beautiful edifice that now houses a remarkable collection of manuscripts and rare books.[12] He notes that the official decree to proceed with the building of a new library and hospital was made in 1757. At that time it was the custom to place a suitable motto over the portal of a library. Duft cites a number of examples of these mottoes, for instance, the quotation from St. Paul (Col. 2:3): "In quo omnes thesauri sapientiae et scientiae," which was used in the libraries of the neighboring monasteries of Wiblingen and of Salem. In choosing an appropriate device for the new St. Gall library, the architect was influenced by the location of the large hall for the collection of books. Since it was adjacent to the infirmary where the physical ills of the community were cared for, it seemed fitting to stress the role of the library in releasing the soul from mental and spiritual ills. Since the greater part of the books were religious—Bibles, works of the Fathers, sermons, lives of the saints, etc.—they could be expected to be efficacious in healing spiritual afflictions as well as securing men against the disease of ignorance in religious matters. So the choice for a motto fell on the one that had been used for the sacred library of Rameses: ΨΥΧΗΣ ΙΑΤΡΕΙΟΝ, "the house of healing for the soul." Happily, the Greek words from Diodorus' text rather than the Latin translation of Poggio—"animi medicamentum"—were chosen.

As in 1760 when the library was built, so today the Greek motto is a focal point of interest at the great hall of the library.[13] Placed above tall doors, the panels of which are outlined in gold, the gilded scroll with the inscription extends across the two wings of the doors. Two marble columns flank the doors and above each is a graceful "putto" who reaches out toward the scroll, directing attention to the motto that indicates the purpose of the library.[14] These two words, in the estimation of book lovers, constitute a perfect memorial to the insight and under-standing of Rameses II and so are of greater significance than all of the material splendor of the great Paris exhibition.

MEDIEVAL METAPHOR AND SYMBOL

THE CLOCK OF ETERNAL WISDOM   Bruxelles, Bibliothèque Royale, MS IV.111, f. 13ʳ

The Clock of Eternal Wisdom

ANCIENT AUTHORS EXHIBITED a high degree of ingenuity in devising metaphors as titles for some of their writings, particularly those that included a variety of separate pieces with a common theme or purpose. Aulus Gellius, in the second century of our era, in his justification of his choice of *Attic Nights* for his miscellaneous collection of essays on a wide variety of topics, commented upon a number of Greek titles that he considered particularly felicitous: *The Muses*, *Athena's Mantle*, *The Horn of Amalthea*, *The Honeycomb*, *Tapestry*, and *Helicon*. By contrast, he noted the less imaginative, nonmetaphorical titles of certain Roman literary works, such as *Natural History*, *Universal History*, and *Moral Epistles*.[1]

Medieval scholars, particularly theologians, were confronted with the same problem of finding suitable titles for their works. Since many of them were concerned with explaining the truths of the Christian religion or in outlining precepts for holy living, appropriate prosaic titles would be severely limited. Fortunately, figurative language was very natural and congenial to the medieval mind. So, for example, in the twelfth century, Peter Riga, a canon of St. Denys, called his great poetic paraphrase of the Bible *Aurora*, for just as the dawn dissipates the darkness of night, so the book, dispelling the obscurities of the Old Testament, glows with the bright light of truth.[2] In like manner, about 1300, a German Dominican prepared a great pictorial presentation of the principal doctrines of Christianity as they are revealed in Scripture and called his work the *Speculum humanae salvationis* [Mirror of human salvation]. This figure of the mirror was used in the fourteenth century by John Gower in his *Speculum hominis, or, Mirour de l'omme* to demonstrate the contest for man's soul by the vices and the virtues. In secular literature it was employed by Vincent of Beauvais for his great encyclopedia of all knowledge—the *Speculum maius*. It continued to be repeated to the time of the Renaissance in such works as the famous *A Mirror for Magistrates*, which reflected the tragedies of English history.

Metaphorical titles for medieval works range from the obvious but very apt *Le Pèlerinage de la Vie humaine* [The pilgrimage of human life], the allegorical poem of Guillaume de Deguilleville, the *Claustrum animae* [The cloister of the soul], widely circulated in religious Houses, the *Hortus deliciarum* [The garden of delights] of Herrad of Landsberg, the anonymous *Turris virtutum* [The tower of virtue], to Jean Meschinot's unique *Lunettes des Princes* [Spectacles for princes], a pleasing variation on the theme of the education of the prince. Among all of these works, one which deserves special notice is a little book written by the Blessed Heinrich Suso which he called *Horologium Sapientiae* [The clock of eternal wisdom].

Born about 1300 in a small village on the shores of Lake Constance, the Dominican friar Heinrich Suso, mystic and poet, disciple of Meister Eckhart, produced what has been named "the finest fruit of German mysticism." The book upon which rests the fame of this "beloved brother" (*Frater amandus*), as he was called by Sapientia herself, was written first, probably about

1335, in German, as *Das Büchlein der ewigen Weisheit*,[3] because, as
he explained in the introduction, it was in that language that
Suso had received these meditations from God. Consisting of
one hundred meditations upon Christ's Passion, the book was
written as the result of a vision vouchsafed to the author after he
had prayed fervently to be freed of the spiritual dryness that had
come upon him.[4] The theme of the meditations is taken from
the *Book of Wisdom* (8.1–2): "Her have I loved, and have sought
her out from my youth, and have desired to take her for my
spouse." It is cast in the form of a dialogue between Eternal
Wisdom and one called the "Servant," who represents Everyman, the ordinary sinful, but contrite, human being yearning for
the love of God.

In his *Büchlein*, Suso expressed his concern over the great
disparity in effectiveness between living, spoken words and silent
words written down on dead parchment, especially those in the
German language, for then their life is lost, they wither like
plucked roses, and consequently they are received in the dryness
of dry hearts.[5] In spite of the author's disclaimer, the book is far
from being lifeless and dull. Written in a Swabian dialect, the
dialogue, as Suso himself pointed out, has a simple message,
expressed simply, by a simple person, for the benefit of simple
people. Yet the author was master of his medium and knew he
must clothe his ideas in figurative language; he was also primarily a poet who sometimes used such poetic devices as
alliteration, metaphor, hyperbole, and on occasion even rhythmi-
cal sentences. The lyrical quality of the language, together with
the fervent outpouring of love for Christ, was largely responsible
for Suso's reputation as *Minnesinger* of *Gottesminne*. The composition of the book was carefully planned for its use as a manual
of devotions. In the colophon Suso gave a stern warning that if
anyone wished to copy the *Büchlein*, he must follow the text
accurately and completely, for Eternal Wisdom herself would
punish anyone who extracted portions of it or otherwise
destroyed the continuity of the work.[6]

It must have been Suso's own earnest desire to share the lively forcefulness of his vision with others that prompted him, several years later, to compose a new version of his book in Latin, a more familiar and a more suitable language for religious teachings and one which would make his message available to a wider circle of readers. He dedicated the new book to the French Master General of the Dominican Order, Hugo de Vaucemain (1333–1341). Suso called his new version the *Horologium Sapientiae*, and composed an introduction to justify the title. There he likened his divine vision to a beautiful clock adorned with lovely roses and fitted with resonant bells that give forth sweet and heavenly tones to move the hearts of all listeners and to quicken their faith.[7] The figure of the clock was not original with Suso, for it occurs as an *exemplum* in contemporary sermons, an emblem of man's soul and body needing regulation for their best performance. Perhaps to reinforce the metaphor, the treatise is divided into twenty-four chapters. It is written in the form of a dialogue between Sapientia (who is at times Eternal Wisdom, the Virgin, and the Word of God) and the Discipulus (who is generally Suso, but also the ordinary bewildered, seeking Christian). Although the author speaks of writing the book as "breaking bread for children,"[8] it is a complex work composed of many themes. Written primarily as a forceful testimonial to furnish those Christians who had experienced spiritual despair with a new spring of joy in the love of God, it also presented strong condemnation of the deterioration of discipline within the Church, of the abuses within the State, and of heresies within the universities. Chiefly, however, it is a book of private devotions and meditations based upon a vibrant mystical experience.

The *Horologium* is not a translation of the *Büchlein*, but rather a complete reworking of the same theme. Some of the original topics are amplified, some completely rearranged; new topics are added, and quotations and further examples from Scripture and the Fathers are cited. Figurative language and visual images are common. The illusion of dialogue is sustained by questions, exclamations, and personal answers. Suso was master of a picturesque and lyrical German style, but he could also write with fluency, clarity, and effectiveness in the more scholarly Latin.

From Constance, the *Horologium* was soon introduced into numerous religious Houses of Orders throughout Germany. It has often been said that in popularity this devotional book was second only to the *De imitatione Christi* of Saint Thomas à Kempis. This claim is substantiated by the great number of manuscript copies of the *Horologium* now preserved in libraries throughout the Continent and in Britain. The earliest were written on vellum, some illuminated with representations of the author and of the clock. These were succeeded by many manuscript copies on paper. A count made about fifty years ago located over two hundred manuscripts of the text.[9] The earliest printed edition appeared in Paris about 1470, followed in 1479 by one in Cologne; in 1487 another edition was printed in Flanders, and in 1492 another appeared in Venice. During this same time, copies of the shorter German *Büchlein* were also being made and circulated throughout Germany. Some scholars have argued that the German version was actually later than the *Horologium*, and was a simplified text for the ordinary monk.[10]

Translations and adaptations of the *Horologium* into the various vernacular languages began to appear before the end of the fourteenth century and continued to be made throughout the fifteenth and sixteenth centuries. In 1966, to mark the sixth centenary of the death of Suso in a commemorative volume on the influence of this great mystic,[11] some attempt was made to take a census of these manuscripts, particularly in France, Holland, Belgium, and Poland, with incidental listings of some copies in Italy and in England. The first French translation, made anonymously by a Franciscan monk in Neufchâteau in 1389, was followed by other French versions. Of these, forty manuscripts located in libraries in France have been recorded.[12] Probably the most beautiful, an elaborately decorated manuscript with thirty-six superb illuminations, is now in the Bibliothèque Royale of Brussels.[13] Between 1578 and 1725, fifteen editions of French translations were printed in France.[14] Of the fifteenth-century Dutch translation, fifty-six copies have been found in libraries chiefly in Holland and Belgium, but also in Germany, England, and France.[15] A census of the works of Suso in Poland includes six manuscripts in Latin and five in Polish, into which the *Horologium* was translated about 1500.[16] A complete register of early versions in English and in Italian and an examination of the copies of these in England and Italy would disclose a large number. The earliest printed edition of the (abridged) English translation appeared about 1490, the first French version in 1493, the first Dutch near the end of the fifteenth century, the first German translation in 1512, and the first Italian in 1642.

There are five manuscripts of the *Horologium* in libraries in the United States. Of these, two are in the Marston collection in the Beinecke Library. One (MS. 130) is an Italian translation, entitled *Orviolo della sapientia*, copied about 1450. It is a thick volume of two hundred and fifty-two leaves of fine vellum, carefully written in a round humanistic script, with wide margins. The large capitals are in delicate penwork in red and blue, and the small capitals are in red. It is bound in the original brown stamped morocco over wooden boards. The volume was obviously prepared for some religious House since, in addition to the text of the *Orviolo*, it contains in Latin the Office of Eternal Wisdom (which was derived from the *Horologium*) and one hundred meditations, followed by instructions in Italian for private devotions fitted to a variety of circumstances. On an opening flyleaf in a later hand there is an undated inscription of ownership indicating that the book belonged to the nuns of Santa Chiara at Murano. It is interesting to note that the Franciscans made extensive use of this devotional written by a Dominican friar.

The other Yale manuscript (Marston MS. 145) is a French translation, also copied about 1450. It is a fine large vellum manuscript of one hundred and eighty leaves. Written in two columns in "bâtarde" script, it has initials, chapter headings, and paragraph marks in red. It is in excellent physical condition and preserves a good text, with occasional corrections by the scribe

himself. Some of the marginal comments were slightly cut away
when the manuscript was trimmed for rebinding. As in many of
the French translations, its colophon gives only the place and
date of the original translation: La ville de Chasteauneuf, 1389.
Except that it was written in France, nothing is known of the
early history of the manuscript. Pasted inside the front cover of
the fine nineteenth-century calf binding is a bookplate of the
library of Maître de Queux de St. Hilaire.

The wide distribution of Suso's book and the long period
during which it continued to be copied and printed give some
indication of the vitality of its message in those troubled times.
Since the age loved allegory, the metaphorical title must have
contributed to its appeal. More unusual than the rather common
"Speculum" and "Hortus," "Horologium" would catch the
attention of the potential reader. Although the author did not
elaborate upon this figure of the clock beyond his explanation in
the preface and a very few casual references in the text, it would
seem likely that he wished to keep before his readers the thought
that God's great truths spoken by Eternal Wisdom are ever alive
like the clock that sounds every hour of the day and night. Suso
was not very precise about this, however, and left his readers to
find their own interpretation. Above all, the juxtaposition of
time and eternity was a theme that all would understand and
recognize as central to the whole religious experience.

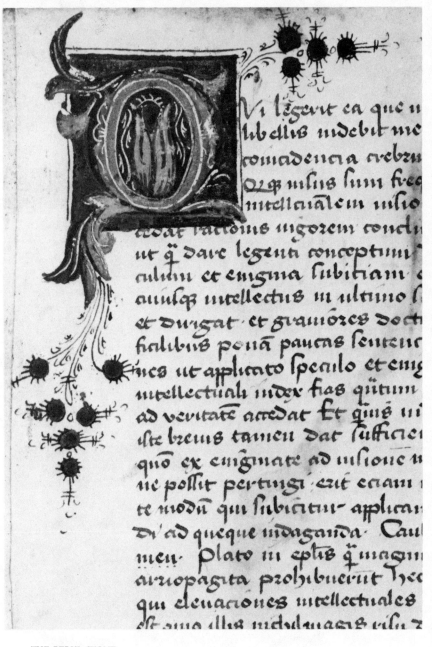

THE BERYL STONE

Beinecke Rare Book and Manuscript Library, Yale University, MS 334, f. 1ʳ

The Mystical Symbol of the Beryl

TWO LARGE HISTORIATED INITIALS on the first folio of a small humanistic manuscript (MS 334) in the Beinecke Library furnish the title of a philosophical text and identify the earliest owner. The first initial of the introduction, a large "Q" in a square background of gold with filigree work in green, blue, and white, which extends above and below the letter, depicts a beryl stone supported on the tips of the petals of a large greenish tulip-shaped flower, indicating that the treatise is the *De beryllo*. With no other reference to the title or the author, the text of chapter one, which explains the origin of the work, begins immediately and continues for two lines on to the *verso* of the folio. Here, in red capitals, the *incipit* is given: "Reverendissimi in christo patris domini Nicolai de Cusa tituli sancti Petri ad vincula Cardinalis presbyteri Berillus feliciter incipit." With the title of work is the name of the author, Cardinal Nicolaus Cusanus or Nicholas of Cues, a native of an ancient town on the Moselle river, who at the time was attached to the Chapter of the Church of San Pietro in Vincoli in Rome.

The second initial, larger than the first, dominates the whole *verso* of the first folio as filigree work and stylized leaves in gold, red, blue, and green extend up to the top and down to the bottom of the page. Within a framework of gold, the letter "B" is set against a blue background, upon which rests a gold shield emblazoned with a crayfish in red and is surmounted by a Cardinal's red hat, the crest of Nicholas of Cues, who had been elevated to the Cardinalate by Pope Nicholas V in 1448. The crayfish represents the family name of Kryfts or Krebs, and of course the hat indicates his ecclesiastical office. The text of chapter two, which is the actual beginning of the treatise, follows with a description of the beryl: "Berillus lapis est lucidus, albus, et transparens...." and continues without a break until the end. The chapters are not numbered but each begins with a red capital initial. The colophon (f. 22^r) supplies the date of the completion of the copying of the manuscript: "Finis, 1459 octava Januarii. Deo laus." Reference to the Church of San Pietro in Vincoli in the *incipit* suggests that it was written in Rome. Both the watermark of the paper (Briquet 6651 from Siena) and the humanistic script confirm the Italian origin of the manuscript. The coat of arms would indicate that it was prepared for the personal use of the author.

The Yale volume has only recently been brought to the attention of scholars.[1] It is composed of twenty-four folios (the last two blank) and is bound in brown calf, blind-stamped with a tooled central panel in geometric designs, with the remains of leather ties. Something of its later history can be determined from several inscriptions on the flyleaves. A date is given on the back endleaf: "Anno domini millezimo quingentezimo vinezimo ottavo die quarta mensis septembris," that is, Sept. 24, 1528. The use of z for c in the numerals and *ottavo* for *octavo* show that it was at that time in the possession of an Italian. On the front flyleaf an inscription, "Bibliotheca del Duque de Sessa" with the date, 1870, reveals that it was owned by a Spanish nobleman. Somewhat later it was in the library of another Spaniard, Ricardo Heredia, whose bookplate is affixed inside the front cover. It was brought to this country by the book collector, Hans P. Kraus, and was donated to Yale by Edwin J. Beinecke in 1965.

Only three other manuscripts of Nicholas of Cues' treatise *De beryllo* have been recorded.[2] They are: *Codex Monacensis latinus 186*, ff. 270^v–292^v, formerly in Tegernsee in Bavaria, now in Munich; *Codex 219*, ff. 199^v–211^v of the Bibliothek des St. Nikolaus-Hospitals in Cues; and *Codex 166*, ff. 422^r–436^v of the Bibliothek des Domgymnasium in Magdeburg. In two important respects the Yale MS 334 differs from the three others. First, it is a small volume containing only the *De beryllo* and it is the only one with illuminated initials, while the others are found in large volumes which include numerous other works of Nicholas. Secondly the Yale manuscript, copied in 1459, is older than the others which are dated 1460–62, 1462, and 1464 respectively, though none of them was derived from the earlier copy. Some errors in spelling and some omissions in the Yale manuscript were neatly corrected by a second hand. Because the manuscript was made for his personal use, it is tempting to look for the hand of Nicholas himself, but there is no evidence of it.[3]

Nicolaus Cusanus (1401–1464), theologian-philosopher, has been credited with being the one systematic and original thinker among the humanists. Trained in theology in Heidelberg and Cologne, with a doctorate in canon law from the University of Padua, he held ecclesiastical positions of great influence, such as that of papal legate to Germany, of delegate to the Council of Basel, of special envoy to Constantinople to try to effect a reconciliation between the Eastern and Western Churches, and of cardinal. As a result of his wide experience in these positions and from his extensive reading in political theory, he wrote a long treatise, *De concordantia catholica*, in which he considers the fundamentals of law and government in Church and society, for the achievement of universal harmony. As a philosopher, Nicholas, trained in Greek and widely read in the Neoplatonists, was especially drawn to the mystical writings attributed to Dionysius the Areopagite and their later interpretations by Eriugena, Bonaventure, and Albertus Magnus. His most significant metaphysical work is the *De docta ignorantia*, an exhaustive treatment of the relativity of knowledge. In discussing the paradox of "learned ignorance," he develops two main themes: that the wise man is learned only when he recognizes the limitations of his reason in comprehending God and his mysteries, and that through the coincidence of opposites, all things are united in God.

The *De beryllo* was composed as a clarification of the *De docta ignorantia*. Because they had difficulty in understanding it, the monks of the Benedictine abbey of St. Quirinus at Tegernsee where Nicholas often visited had written to him begging for a summary in simple language.[4] In the long essay he wrote to comply with their request, Nicholas used the analogy of the mystical lens of the beryl as the key to the whole problem. The clear, white, transparent stone with its convex and concave sides serves as a magnifying lens by which the finite human eye can see the invisible. In like manner, by means of intellectual vision the finite human mind is able to perceive the suprarational and so to apprehend in some imperfect way the mysteries of God and the universe. Nicholas repeats the figure of the beryl throughout to symbolize the inner vision as he expounds such elemental subjects as the first principle, unity, being, substance, and man, all of which he calls *aenigmata* that have puzzled man throughout history. On all of these questions he gives the opinions of the philosophers from Pythagoras, Plato, and Aristotle to Avicenna and Thomas Aquinas, then clearly states his own agreement or disagreement with them.

The figure of the beryl stone was ideal for Nicholas' purpose. Like some of the other precious stones which had been associated with magic from ancient times, the beryl was thought to exert a salutary influence upon men and was regarded by such authorities as Marbode of Rennes (1035–1123)[5] and Albertus Magnus (1206?–1280)[6] as beneficial in curing some of men's physical ills. Yet even the testimony of these specialists did not interest the scientific mind of Nicholas,[7] for he simply describes the stone as clear and transparent so that the color would not obtrude upon any object. Since the stone occurs in nature as a hexagonal prism, its sides would naturally direct the light toward the center, and, according to Nicholas, have such magnifying power as to make visible the invisible.[8]

Nicholas was a keen mathematician, and throughout his treatise he uses the methods of geometry with geometric diagrams to clarify his propositions. One might then expect to find his illustration of the beryl stone in the form of a scientific sketch, but the artist who illuminated the manuscript used symbolic language. The beryl crystal, which represents intellectual vision, is painted resting upon a great flower which stands for what is transitory and superficial. Only by the aid of inner vision can one look through the external and temporal to the eternal and unchanging verities.[9]

The Symbol of the Y of Pythagoras
in the Ninth Century

THE ALLEGORY OF THE PILGRIMAGE OF LIFE had a particular appeal for the men of the Renaissance.[1] Among the many versions in which the allegory was presented, those which had as their theme the choice offered by diverging ways were the most popular, perhaps because they had the prestige of an origin in classical literature, because their message was entirely consistent with Christian ethic,[2] and because they lent themselves to striking graphic representations. The three best-known variations on the theme of the Choice of Two Ways are: the Choice of Heracles, first related by Xenophon in his *Memorabilia* where he credits the myth to the sophist Prodicus;[3] the *Tablet* of Cebes, probably written in the first century of our era, though it was long thought to have been the work of a friend of Socrates;[4] and the Y of Pythagoras,[5] which was Greek in origin and became associated with Neopythagoreanism in the East,[6] but was introduced into Western literature by the Roman satirist, Persius.[7]

In the first of these allegories, Heracles has come to a crossroad in his life and is trying to decide upon the future course of his journey, when he is confronted by two ladies: Pleasure (also bluntly called Vice) and Virtue. Each tries to persuade him to follow her, Pleasure to a life of gaiety and ease, and Virtue to the rigors of a life of duty and responsibility. Cebes presents his allegory in the form of a scene depicted upon a votive tablet set before a shrine of Saturn where a wise Old Man interprets it to passersby. On the tablet pilgrims on the road of life are faced again and again with a choice of diverging ways as they are lured by such deceptive ladies as Lust, Deceit, Avarice, and False Learning from the steep path which leads to Happiness and True Knowledge. The Y of Pythagoras, as it has come down to us, is a symbol rather than a myth. The stem of the Y represents protected infancy and childhood; where the two arms branch from the stem there is indicated the critical period when a boy is growing into manhood and must make a choice between the two ways. The steep path to the right leads to a life of virtue, but the easier path to the left leads to a life of evil and destruction. The symbol is, of course, a somewhat elaborate parallel to the scene presented by Virgil in the sixth book of the *Aeneid* when the Sibyl, conducting the hero through the Under-world, points to the crossways and says that the path to the right leads to Elysium, while the one to left leads to pitiless Tartarus.[8] It is also akin to Christ's injunction, "Enter ye in at the strait gate: for wide is the gate and broad is the way, that leadeth to destruction (Matt. 7: 13–14).

Contrary to what one might have expected, of the three versions of the allegory of the Choice of Ways, it was the last, the Y of Pythagoras, that had a continuous history from ancient times to the Renaissance, while the two more colorful, more detailed accounts disappeared after classical times and were only restored by the humanists. Isolated references to the Y of Pythagoras, generally deriving from a passage in Lactantius' *Divinae institutiones* (VI.3), are found throughout the Middle Ages, largely in hagiographical writings such as Walter of Spire's *Vita sancti Christophori* (IV.232–233) in the eleventh century, but also in secular texts like William of Malmesbury's *Gesta regum*

Anglorum (III.167) in the twelfth.[9] Yet credit for passing on an explanation of the Pythagorean letter must be given in large part to the school of St. Germain of Auxerre in the ninth century,[10] and specifically to its two great teachers, Heiric and Remigius. During the reign of Charles the Bald this school was considered the best in the Frankish kingdom. Its reputation was largely built up through the talents and accomplishments of the great teacher, Heiric,[11] who died in 876. Having studied at Ferrières under the learned Lupus and at Laon with several of the Irish scholars there, he came to teach at Auxerre with a wide acquaintance with Latin texts and a knowledge of many of the encyclopedic works of late antiquity. His great concern was to accumulate a library of classical texts and to teach the classical authors, in addition to giving the monks a sound training in Biblical exegesis. Heiric's most able student and his successor as head of the school was Remigius, who survived him by twenty-three years.[12] Untiring in his zeal for teaching, Remigius carried on the tradition established by Heiric in expounding an extraordinary number of literary texts, works on grammar, Biblical texts, and books on dogma. After 883, he went to Rheims to help restore the school there and in 900 to Paris where he won acclaim by his lectures on the seven liberal arts.

It was at the school of Auxerre, however, that the symbol of the Y of Pythagoras was made known to an ever-widening group of students. Both Heiric and Remigius expounded the difficult poetry of the first-century Stoic satirist, Persius. Twice in his poems, Persius mentions the symbol. In Satire III he inveighs against the stupidity of privileged young men who seem to have no goal in life, living from one moment to the next, even though they have had the advantage of studying the doctrines of the philosophers, particularly the Stoics. Persius, in lines 56–57, denounces them and reminds them that they also know that the letter Y "which spreads out into Pythagorean branches has pointed out to you the steep path which rises to the right." In Satire V, lines 34–35, Persius writes a charming tribute to his teacher, Cornutus, into whose care he placed himself, "at the age when the path of life is doubtful, and wandering, ignorant of life, parted my trembling soul into the branching crossways." He must have assumed that his readers would know the symbol of the Y of Pythagoras, for he fails to mention two important points: the letter he refers to is Y, and the steep right branch is the one to be chosen, for it leads to happiness, while the left branch is wider and less difficult, but leads to destruction. Since the young pupils at the school of Auxerre would not understand the references, it was the particular responsibility of the teachers to explain the passages.

Heiric and Remigius not only assembled as many of the commentaries and encyclopedic works as they could, but they also made good use of them. There were at least three of these works where they would have found the Y of Pythagoras mentioned. The fourth-century grammarian, Servius, in his great commentary on the *Aeneid*, explains the symbol very satisfactorily: "We know that Pythagoras of Samos divided human life into the semblance of the letter Y, because in the first part of it the individual is uncertain and has not yet given himself to either vices or virtues. The branching of the letter Y, however, begins in the time of youth, when the boy chooses to follow either the vices, that is, the left branch, or the virtues, that is, the right." [13] The second reference, the fifth-century encyclopedia of the seven liberal arts compiled by Martianus Capella, is not an explanation, but simply a circumlocution for the letter Y: "the letter which the wise Samian thought represented the two ways of life." [14] The third compilation discussing the question is the *Etymologiae* of Isidore of Seville, assembled in the seventh century. In his treatment of the alphabet, for the letter Y, he follows Servius or Servius' source, using some of the same phrases. He says, "Pythagoras of Samos first fashioned the letter Y after the pattern of human life. The lower part, the stem, signifies the first period when the individual has not yet committed himself to either virtues or vices. The branching of the ways, however, begins in adolescence. The right branch is steep, but it leads to a happy life, while the left is easier, but it leads to destruction."[15] He then quotes the passage in Persius III,56. Such were the resources available to the two teachers to explain Pythagoras to their pupils.

Some of the lecture notes of both Heiric and Remigius have been preserved, and among these there are several references to the Y of Pythagoras. A body of comments on the poems of Persius, now known as the "vulgate scholia", occurs in a tenth-century manuscript. Though this seems to represent an accumulation of notes from more than one source, it is thought that the bulk of the comments are those of Heiric.[16] The gloss on Persius III.56 reads: "Not unknown to you are the teachings of Pythagoras who was born on the island of Samos. He invented the letter Y which he likened to human life which in infancy is not yet divided because of the admonitions of teacher or fear of father. But after an individual has come to adolescence, he is faced with a choice. The branch [of the letter] to the left represents vices that afford an easy access because they are on the downward slope. On the other hand, the right branch where works of virtue are honored opens on a difficult and steep path, but whoever has passed over it is received into the happy abode. One of those (opposite) ends anyone from his sixteenth year will achieve once he has set his course. In like manner he said that through vices one comes quickly to destruction, but one attains to happiness through virtues only slowly."[17] Heiric also made reference to the Y of Pythagoras in his long poem on the *Life of St. Germanus* (I.79–84). In speaking of the youth of the saint, he says that at a time when young children are as yet unmarked by a single blemish, when their minds are like wax to be fashioned, and when the branching ways of the Pythagorean letter lead to opposite paths, when lack of resolve makes one hesitate to choose the right and evil influences urge the left path, "then the steeper way seemed best to him."[18]

Compared with the explanations of Heiric, Remigius' notes on the Y of Pythagoras seem more stereotyped and unimaginative. There are at least three instances where Remigius explains the symbol, and all are derived from Servius and Isidore of Seville.

In a comment on Bede's *De arte metrica*, he gives the familiar explanation: "Pythagoras of Samos fashioned the letter Y into a semblance of human life. The stem of the letter represents the uncertainty of childhood which has not given itself either to virtues or to vices. The parting of the way begins in adolescence: the right branch is hard and steep, but it leads to a happy life, while the left is easy but it leads to sin and death."[19] Essentially the same gloss occurs in Remigius' commentary on *Ars de nomine et verbo* by the grammarian, Phocas.[20] There is a little variation in his Commentary on Martianus Capella where he is glossing the very ambiguous reference to the Y. He explains: "Pythagoras fashioned the Y into the form of human life, whence Persius says, '[it] parted my trembling soul in the branching crossways.' For the letter Y begins with a single stem which is divided into a kind of double way. So in childhood man's nature is simple and it is not easy to discern whether he will choose the good or the evil way. In youth, however, he chooses either the virtues which are designated by the shorter and steeper branch, or he turns to the side of the vices which are represented by the left, that is the wider branch."[21]

Since Martianus Capella's great encyclopedia of the seven liberal arts was used as a textbook throughout Europe for hundreds of years, and since it was impossible for an ordinary teacher to use it without some assistance, the commentary of Remigius soon had a very wide circulation. As the extant manuscripts ranging from the tenth to the sixteenth century are found in libraries throughout Europe, it would seem that few educated persons in the Middle Ages would not have heard of Remigius' explanation of the Y of Pythagoras. If, during all this time, the Y was written as a normal roman Y, as indeed it appears in the manuscripts, it seems strange that no one questioned certain details of the symbol. The roman letter Y has two branches which seem identical except that in some cases one branch is slightly wider than the other. Both are joined to the stem at the same angle, and both are the same length, so that, without exterior influences, there would seem to be no reason for a person to choose one way rather than the other. Yet the

LE TIERS LIVRE. FEVIL. LXIII.

COntemplez icy le gracieulx & beau Festi que ie vous ay faict, o ieunes & bons amateurs de Vertus, & y prenez bien garde commant a la pante de la voye de volupte ie ay figure & atache vne espee, vng foit, des verges, vng gibet, & vng feu. pour monstrer quen fin de Volupte dependent & sensuyuent tous miserables maulx & griefz torments. Du coste de la voye de Vertus, ie y ay faict vne aultre pante, ou iay mis & atache en desseing & figure, vng chapeau de Laurier, des Palmes, des Sceptres, & vne Corône, pour bailler a cognoistre & a entendre, que de Vertus vient toute gloire pure, tout pris, tout honneur, & toute royalle domination.

Sens moral de la lettre Pythagorique.

GEOFFROY TORY'S PRINTER'S DEVICE, THE Y OF PYTHAGORAS. GEOFFROY TORY, *Champfleury* (Paris, 1529), P. LXIII

Beinecke Rare Book and Manuscript Library, Yale University

explanations insist that the right branch is much steeper and more difficult than the left; the left branch is wider, easier to traverse, and hence more inviting, though it is longer. One cannot avoid the conclusion that the original Y of the symbol was different from the roman Y which was used throughout the Middle Ages. In his edition of Persius, commenting on III.56–57, the eminent classicist, J. Conington, made the suggestion[22] that the letter described by Persius, following his unidentified predecessors, was the early form of the letter upsilon Ч. This letter has a straight stem which continues straight and steep to the end, but branching from it to the left is a rounded arm that makes a gentle and generous curve before turning upwards. This would mean that the life represented by the right shaft is altogether straight and steep, while the life represented by the left has a pleasant and easy path before the final steep climb and the distance covered is longer. If this explanation was known to the school of Auxerre, they left no indication of it.

The origin of the Y of Pythagoras has not been determined. Diogenes Laertius, the second-century biographer of the Greek philosophers, in a full account of Pythagoras, fails to metion the Y.[23] Of course the idea was very old, as one sees in Hesiod's *Works and Days* where the poet warns the lazy Perses of the two roads that lead, one to Goodness and the other to Badness,[24] yet no precise description of the symbol in early times has survived or even been mentioned. On the other hand, the eventual transformation of the symbol is well-known and dramatic, as men of the Renaissance saw in the Pythagorean Y a splendid subject for pictorial representation.[25] The most noteworthy artist to use the theme was the famous French scholar, calligrapher, and printer, Geoffroy Tory. In 1529 he produced a treatise on the roman capital letters which has become a classic. In this *Champfleury* the letter Y is represented as the symbol of Pythagoras.[26] The plain roman Y is placed within a large laurel wreath and is supported by two ribbons which secure the two arms of the letter just below their broadened surfaces. From the narrower right arm of the letter, a series of insignia of rewards is suspended: a laurel wreath, two crossed palm branches, a scepter, a book, and finally a large crown. From the broader left arm hang insignia of punishment: a sword, a scourge, rods, a gibbet, and a blazing fire. Beneath is the artist's explanation of the symbol. Tory must have been especially pleased with this version of the letter Y, for he used a variation of it as a printer's device in a number of the books published at his press. An engraving of the device is given in the famous emblem book of Zacharias Heyns.[27] Here a great Y stands alone on a plain against a background of distant mountains. For some unexplained reason,[28] the branches of the letter are reversed from the usual pattern. The wide branch is on the right, and from its upper surface flames rise high into the air, while objects of defeat are suspended: a sword, a gibbet, and a wheel. The narrow branch on the left is topped by a large crown and symbols of victory are hanging from it: an orb, a scepter, a palm leaf, and a book.

So, in the end, the simple Y of Pythagoras, which in the Middle Ages had become stereotyped as an academic metaphor of the two ways of life, finally became the subject of pictorial representations to vie with those illustrating the more famous allegories of the Choice of Heracles and the *Tablet* of Cebes.

THE UNEXPECTED IN MANUSCRIPTS

SEnatui populoq̄ romano. / Lentulus sal. D. Apparuit / temporibus istis: et adhuc / est homo magne virtutis / nominatus xp̄ianus iesus: / qui dicitur a gentibus pro / pheta veritatis: que eius / discipuli vocant filium dei: / Suscitans mortuos: et sanal / eos. Longores. Homo quidem / stature procerus: mediocris / ce spectabilis: vultu habens / uenerabilem. Que intuētes / possūt diligere: et formidare: / Capillos habens coloris nucis / auellane premature: et pla / nos fere usq; ad aures: ab / auribus vero cincinnos crī / spos: aliquantulu ceruliores:

& fulgentiores

et flocentiores ab humeris / uentilantes: discrimē hn̄s / in medio capitis: iuxta morē / nazareoru: frontē planaz: / et serenissimaz cū facie si / ne ruga et macula aliq̄ue / quā rubor moderatus uenustat, / nasi et oris nulla prorsus / est reprensio: barbā h n̄s / copiosaz: et impuberē capil / lis concolorez: nō longaz: Sed / i medio bifurcataz: Aspectū / habens simplicē: et maturū, / oculis glaucis: uarijs et cla / ris existentibus: Jn increpa / tione terribilis: In admoni / tione blandus: et amabilis / et h ilaris: seruata gra / uitate: qui nunq̄; uisus ē

The Letter of Lentulus
Describing Christ

THE PERSISTENT TRADITION of an authentic portrait of Christ made during his lifetime was given new vitality in the fifteenth century by the discovery and circulation of a letter purporting to have been written to the Roman Senate during the reign of Tiberius Caesar by Publius Lentulus, procurator of Judea. In the Beinecke Library there is a manuscript, written in Italy in the fifteenth century (Marston MS 49), that contains this Latin epistle of Publius Lentulus, preceded by the text of Donatus' Life of Virgil. The letter gives a detailed description of the physical appearance and general bearing of Christ, as well as the impression he made upon those who came into his presence. Two additional versions of the letter, both in Italian translation, are found in other, roughly contemporary, Yale manuscripts. One occurs in a Florentine miscellany, dated about 1460 (Marston MS 247), among a group of letters and orations of Petrarch, Boccaccio, Filelfo, and other Italian scholars; the second is part of a comparable Renaissance miscellany of letters of the hu-

49

manists, copied about 1440 (MS 329). A fourth version, in Latin, appears in a small volume written in Austria in 1485, now in the James Marshall and Marie-Louise Osborn Collections (MS a 7). The letter of Lentulus appears also in two early printed books in the Beinecke Library: an Italian translation is included among the devotional poems, the *Laudi* (Venice, 1514), of the thirteenth-century mystic Jacopone da Todi; the Latin version occurs in a collection of moral and philosophical treatises printed in Padua in 1535. That one library should have so many versions of the Lentulus letter suggests its phenomenal popularity, especially in Italy in the fifteenth century. There are no complete statistics, but almost a century ago a German scholar listed seventy-five manuscripts, chiefly in Germany and France.[1]

Since neither the Gospels nor the Epistles make any mention of the physical characteristics of Christ, the idealized word picture contained in Lentulus' letter was presumably created originally by the profound desire of some devout Christian for a visual image of the Founder. Ironically enough, just about the time the letter was being dispersed so widely in Italy, the fearless critic Lorenzo Valla denounced it as a fraud in his famous treatise (composed about 1440) exposing the Donation of Constantine.[2] Yet even after that, the letter was given greater prestige by being incorporated into the prologue of the *Meditationes in vitam Christi* of Ludolphus of Saxonia in the printed edition (Nuremberg, 1483) of this popular work originally written in the mid-fourteenth century. In a similar way it was printed in the introductory letter, from Johannes Loffelholtz to Petrus Danhuser, in a collection of the writings of the eleventh-century Saint Anselme of Canterbury (Nuremberg, 1491). (Neither Ludolphus nor Anselme had had any knowledge of the letter.) Later, in the sixteenth century, it was printed as authentic by the great Protestant theologian Matthias Flacius, Illyricus, in his monumental *Ecclesiastica historia*, commonly known as the *Centuries of Magdeburg*.[3] It continued to appear, most often as a single text, as late as the end of the last century,[4] and is now included among the texts of the Apocryphal New Testament.[5]

Evidence concerning the origin of the letter occurs in a manuscript in the Library of the University of Jena.[6] In a fifteenth-century collection of miscellaneous theological works, the Lentulus letter appears as the eleventh item, and bears an interesting colophon:

> Explicit epistola Iacobi de Columpna, anno domini 1421, reperta in annalibus Romae, in libro antiquissimo in Capitolio, doct. domino Patriarchae Constantinopolitano.

This would indicate that a member of the famous Roman Colonna family had found it inserted in a very old book of the Annals of Rome. If, indeed, the letter had been sent much earlier by the Patriarch of Constantinople, it would certainly have been written originally in Greek. It would seem reasonable to think that some Italian humanist, perhaps as much as a century earlier, had translated the letter into Latin. At any rate the Latin epistle discovered by Jacopo Colonna in 1421 must have created a sensation that would account for the rapid multiplication of copies. It would also explain why it was unknown in the West before this time.

Before exploring the antecedents of the letter in its Greek sources, I shall translate the text as it occurs in Yale manuscript Marston MS 49:

> Lentulus, to the Senate and the Roman people, greetings.
>
> There has appeared in these times, and, indeed, is still living, a man of great power named Christ Jesus, who is said by the Gentiles to be the prophet of truth, but his disciples call him the Son of God. He raises the dead and heals all diseases. He is a man of average size and pleasing appearance, having a countenance that commands respect, which those who behold may love or fear. He has hair the color of an unripe hazelnut, smooth almost to his ears, but below his ears curling and rather darker and more shining, hanging over his shoulders, and having a parting in the middle of his head

according to the fashion of the Nazarenes. His brow is smooth and quite serene; his face is without wrinkle or blemish, and a slight ruddiness makes it handsome. No fault can be found with his nose and mouth; he has a full beard of the color of his hair, not long but divided in two at the chin. His facial expression is guileless and mature; his eyes are grayish and clear. In his rebukes he is terrible, but in his admonitions he is gentle and kind; he is cheerful but always maintains his dignity. At times he has wept, but he has never laughed. In stature he is tall and erect and his hands and arms are fine to behold. His speech is grave, reserved, and temperate, so that he is rightly called by the prophet, "Fairer than the sons of men." Ps. 45: 2

This is the end of the letter that Lentulus sent to the Senate and the Roman people, concerning the appearance of our Lord Jesus Christ.

It would seem, to judge by the attention given to detail and particularly to colors, that this aprocryphal letter may, in its original form, have been composed in the presence of some portrait of Christ. No Greek original for the letter is known to exist, but there are at least three passages in earlier Greek writings which give similar descriptions. Closest in time to the Lentulus letter is that found in the fourteenth-century *Ecclesiastical History* of Nicephorus Callistus, in a section entitled: "On the divine and human features of our Saviour, Jesus Christ."[7] With the prefatory "As we have learned from the ancients," the author notes a number of significant details: blond hair, thick, and falling into waves over the shoulders; dark eyebrows; short blond beard; eyes dark and remarkably kindly, but sharp; light complexion, slightly ruddy; face showing gravity, prudence, and gentleness, very like his Mother.

Another description, probably first set down in the eleventh century, was edited in the eighteenth century by the monk, Dionysius of Phurna, in a *Handbook of Painting*,[8] a guide to Christian iconography that treats of the methods and materials of painting and the works of art from Mount Athos. It occurs in a section entitled: "On the countenance and form of our Lord as we have learned it from those who have seen him with their own eyes." Here the author mentions gentleness as the salient characteristic of the face. He also notes: beautiful eyebrows that meet; lovely eyes; beautiful white nose; complexion like ripe grain; curly golden hair; dark beard; fingers long and slender; gentle bearing, very like his Mother.

An eighth-century description of Christ is found in the works of St. John of Damascus, in his *Epistola ad Theophilum*.[9] Here the details include: beautiful eyes, with eyebrows that meet; straight nose; curly hair; pleasant voice; gentle, serene, and patient manner.

In spite of the differences, the repetition and similarities suggest that all three accounts, along with the Lentulus letter, may stem from a common source;[10] and, indeed, all may be descriptions derived from the same idealized portrait. What the ultimate origin of such a likeness may have been is suggested in another work of St. John of Damascus, the *De imaginibus oratio*.[11] Here John reports the existence of a miraculous impression of the face of Christ, sent by Christ himself, just before his death, to Abgarus, King of Edessa.[12]

This portrait is an important part of the whole Abgarus legend. About A.D. 200, an unknown person, perhaps to give emphasis to the early conversion of the Mesopotamian kingdom of Edessa to Christianity, fabricated two letters in Syriac. One of them purported to have been written by King Abgarus Uchomo to Jesus, asking him to come to Edessa to heal him of a grave illness and there to find refuge from persecution. The other is the answer of Jesus, telling the king that the end is near and he is unable to go, but that later one of the disciples will go to Edessa and cure the king's disease. These two letters were seen by the historian Eusebius, who regarded them as genuine and translated them into Greek.[13] From this basis the legend was expanded to include a story that with his letter Abgarus sent a messenger, Ananias, with instructions to paint a portrait of Christ. When, however, the painter attempted to delineate the features, he was so dazzled by the brilliance emanating from the divine countenance that he could not continue. Thereupon Christ took a linen cloth and pressing it to his face produced a marvellous likeness, which Ananias took back to Edessa. This portrait was a treasured possession of the king (who was cured by St. Thomas), and it provided a miraculous protection for the city.[14] According to tradition, it was sent in 944 to the Emperor Constantine Porphyrogenitus in Constantinople, where it was the object of great veneration. Eventually, when Constantinople fell, the portrait was taken to Rome and placed in the Church of St. Sylvester.[15]

Of all the witnesses to the existence of the miraculous picture, the most reliable would seem to be the historians. Evagrius, for one, in the seventh century, in his *Ecclesiastical History*,[16] cites Procopius for evidence of the "God-made image" which successfully protected Edessa against the Persian King Chostroes. In the record of the Second Council of Nicaea (Seventh Synod), held in 787, there is a letter purporting to have been written in 726 by Pope Gregory II to the Emperor Leo III, the Isaurian, on the subject of the iconoclastic movement headed by Leo. The Pope, reminding Leo of the Abgarus-Jesus letters and the miraculous portrait, bids him go to Edessa and behold the venerable image of Christ "that was not made by human hands, worshipped and adored by multitudes of the people in the East."[17] A third witness to the portrait is a long narrative, attributed to the Emperor Constantine Porphyrogenitus,[18] of the whole history of the letters and the sacred image to the time they were taken from Edessa to Constantinople in 844. In it several incidents are added. For example, when the messenger Ananias, on his way to Edessa, stopped in Hierapolis, the inhabitants of that city were determined to keep the holy relic. Miraculously, a duplicate was made, which they kept and zealously guarded. In Edessa the original was considered the most precious possession of the kingdom, yet the Emperor was able to prevail upon the people to send it to Constantinople. Described in detail are solemn ceremonies, the religious procession, the numerous stops at holy places en route, and the emotional reception of the marvelous relic in Constantinople by the clergy, the Emperor, and the people. The account states specifically that the portrait was placed briefly upon the imperial throne, where the Emperor viewed it and reverenced it, before its enshrinement in a church for the eternal protection of the realm. As a final witness, in the twelfth century, Zonaras in his *Annales*,[19] chronicling the tempestuous times following the death of Constantine, and speaking of the Emperor Nicephorus Phocas (963–969) in his campaign to recover Cyprus and Syria, says that in Hierapolis his soldiers found the duplicate of the miraculous portrait of Christ and brought it back to Constantinople.

One can only conclude that, whatever its origin, there was an early portrait of Christ that men of the East believed to have been made in a miraculous manner during Christ's lifetime and which they guarded and reverenced. Further, three descriptions of an early portrait agree in many details and must all derive from a common source. Hence, the letter of Lentulus, apocryphal though it is, also belongs in the tradition.

As an epilogue, it may not be inappropriate to cite two passages from the remarkable *Handbook of Painting* from Mount Athos which show clearly the vitality of the tradition. Since the *Handbook* was compiled to furnish young painters with both the techniques of making religious paintings and the precise directions for the accepted representations of all the personages they would be called upon to paint, the compiler added a section of preliminary instructions for the mental and spiritual preparation of the artist. These include a prayer to God, a hymn to the Virgin, and a prayer to Christ, recognizing his divine and human natures. This last recalls Christ's particular relevance for artists in the clause,

> you who have deigned to delineate the sacred character of your immortal countenance and to imprint it upon a holy linen cloth, which served to cure the disease of the satrap Abgarus, and to enlighten his soul for the acceptance of the true God.[20]

After the prayer, the author enjoins upon the young student the necessity of devoting himself tirelessly to acquiring the skills necessary for his work. He impresses upon the novice that his art, which God himself had taught men, is divinely sanctioned, a fact that is substantiated especially

> by the existence of the venerable portrait not made by human hands, upon which Jesus Christ imprinted his sacred countenance on a linen cloth which, as an exact and divine image of his countenance, he sent to Edessa to the satrap Abgarus.[21]

The "Gentle Puritan"
and the "Angelic Doctor"

FEW COLLEGE PRESIDENTS have ever had greater or more varied
responsibilities or undertaken a wider range of related activities
than Ezra Stiles when he was President of Yale College. In
addition to his manifold administrative tasks, he taught Hebrew
to all of the students and was Professor of Ecclesiastical History.
Besides these regular appointments he often gave lectures on
optics, astronomy, mathematics, geography, natural philosophy,
and other subjects. As a lawyer, he had numerous obligations to
the college, the community, and the state; as a minister he often
preached in the college chapel and in various churches and
performed other pastoral duties. For the students he served as
chief examiner of the entering classes and as judge of their
competence for promotion and graduation. Between the dis-
charge of these functions and his frequent journeys throughout
Connecticut and into Massachusetts and New York, he somehow
found time to read a great number of books: in his *Diary* he
mentions reading Tertullian, Josephus, Eusebius, Origen,

ILLUSTRATION OF JACOB'S DREAM FROM THE *Speculum humanae salvationis*
Beinecke Rare Book and Manuscript Library, Yale University, MS 27, f. 61^v

Clement of Alexandria, and Justin Martyr, as well as contemporary books in every field, including Mary Wollstonecraft's
recently published *Rights of Women*.[1] So it is not surprising that
Stiles took the opportunity to read a Latin treatise in an old
manuscript in the Yale Library, signing his name with the date,
26 January 1793, and noting: "Perlegi hunc Librum." (I have
read this book through.)[2]

The large volume in which President Stiles made his notation
is one of Yale's treasures. Of the forty books given to the college
by Governor Elihu Yale in 1714, this was the only medieval
manuscript. In Jeremiah Dummer's list of books from several
donors which he consigned to the college from England, it is
designated: "A Curious Ancient Manuscript. fol."[3] The volume,
bound in its original pigskin wrapper over wooden boards,
consists of one hundred and four leaves of heavy vellum, and
seems to have been written and bound in England about 1400.
The text is in Gothic script in black ink; ornamental initials are
in blue and red with elaborate penwork in red, and the chapter
headings and titles are also in red. It has one hundred sixty-two
pen-and-ink drawings, six others having been cut out. The first
seventy-one leaves contain the text of the *Speculum humanae
salvationis* [Mirror of man's salvation]; the last thirteen leaves
have a devotional text, "Meditationes de passione Domini,"
once attributed to St. Bonaventure.

The *Speculum* was one of the most effective teaching devices
ever created by medieval clerics for the instruction of the laity in
the central message of the Christian religion. Preceded in the
twelfth century by Peter Comestor's *Historia scholastica*, in which
all of the Old and New Testament history, along with legends of
the saints, was set forth in simple language, and followed slightly
later by Peter Riga's *Aurora*, a versified Bible, the *Speculum*
presents the same great drama, but in pictorial form. Comparable
in purpose to the popular *Biblia pauperum* [Poor Man's Bible],
which was written in Germany about 1300, the *Speculum* also
includes pertinent material from secular history and saints' lives.
As presented in the Yale manuscript, it is introduced by an

elaborate analytical index and a "Prohemium" of one hundred lines in verse explaining the purpose of the book—to teach the unlearned by means of pictures. There follow forty-two chapters, each of a hundred verses, and each illustrated by four drawings. The first two chapters are devoted to the Old Testament and portray the fall of the angels, the creation of man, his temptation and fall—all clearly showing man's need for redemption. The rest of the treatise is devoted to the New Testament, depicting the birth of the Virgin, the birth and passion of Christ, Pentecost, the last judgment, the pains of hell, and the joys of heaven. In each chapter, the first text and drawing are concerned with a scene from the life of Christ, while the other three texts and drawings illustrate comparable scenes from the Old Testament or secular history as they prefigure the parallel Christian episode. The main text is followed by three additional chapters on the Seven Hours of the Passion, the Seven Sorrows and the Seven Joys of Mary.

The *Speculum* originated in Germany, probably from the region of Strassburg, about 1300. Neither the author nor the date is revealed in the treatise,[4] but the sympathetic treatment of three Dominican saints, Dominic, Peter Martyr, and Thomas Aquinas, and the general flavor of Dominican teaching would indicate that it was composed by a member of the Dominican Order. The work was copied very widely in the fourteenth and fifteenth centuries and well over two hundred manuscripts are still in existence.[5] It was first printed by Gunther Zainer in Augsburg before 1473, and shortly thereafter translations were made into German and English.

When Ezra Stiles read this treatise through, what did he know of its place in the Christian tradition? Fortunately two sources supply information on this point. The first is Stiles' *Diary*, where, under date of 16 December 1792, he writes:

> Reading the antient MS. on Christ's Passion sent to the Coll. Library by Gov. Yale abot 1714. It is probably 500 years old, certainly since the Times of St. Francis & St. Dominic who lived A.D. 1216, as their Names are mentioned. It is a romish Treatise on Theology.[6]

There are eight later notations (17, 23, 27, 28 December, 12, 13, 20, and 26 January) where he mentions briefly that he is continuing to read the book. The next-to-the-last notation adds: "The Author mentions Tho. Aquinas." The manuscript itself is the second source of information. Besides the note with Stiles' signature at the end, there are two other comments in his handwriting and signed with his name. In the right margin of the *recto* of leaf 78 he writes: "So this MS composed & written since A.D. 1250 when Aquinas flourished." And in the lower margin of the *recto* of leaf 90 he writes: "This MS composed since Thomas Aquinas A.D. 1250 containing...." (The rest of the note, which apparently consisted of four statements, has been erased and is now illegible.) Although Stiles, in giving the age of the manuscript as "probably 500 years," made a natural mistake in equating the time of composition with the date of the Yale copy, he was correct in thinking that the text represents the Dominican point of view and particularly that it is in the tradition of St. Thomas Aquinas.

It is interesting to conjecture why Stiles, a Congregational minister, in the midst of his responsibilities as President of Yale, took the time to read a "romish Treatise on Theology." First of all, he had an insatiable thirst for knowledge of every kind which drove him to read in many diverse fields of scholarship and particularly in far-from-sectarian theology and religious philosophy. This is evidenced in the numerous entries in his *Diary* of his reading and translating of the mystical writings, the *Celestial Hierarchy* and the *Divine Names*, attributed to Dionysius the Areopagite, whom Stiles once called "my beloved Dionysius."[7] Secondly, as Professor of Ecclesiastical History, Stiles would have felt obligated to understand the various steps in the development of Christian theology. This would have necessitated his acquaintance with the doctors of the Church and the medieval theologians, however much he might wish to emphasize the Protestant point of view. In the bitter quarrels within his own denomination, Stiles did not become a militant adversary of any dissenting group. In 1752 and again in 1754, he was offered the post of rector of the Anglican parish in Newport. Later, while serving as Congregational minister in that city, he frequently attended services in the local synagogue, and in learning Hebrew he often consulted the rabbi. He counted himself a friend to ministers of many Protestant denominations and during his various journeys to other communities made a point of attending services in different churches, including the Catholic and the Quaker. He seems to have felt a kind of ecumenicity rare in his day; as he himself phrased it, he "professed a universal Charity."[8]

Against this background, it would seem as if Stiles' labeling of the *Speculum* as "romish" was not derogatory, but merely descriptive. He had, for example, studied with appreciation the great *Summa theologica* of that most eminent of Catholic theologians, St. Thomas Aquinas. In an unusual entry in his *Diary* he gives an indication of his reaction to the Dominican's clear and logical exposition of Christian theology when he remarks that in another generation even the valuable writings of President Jonathan Edwards may well pass into near-oblivion and that when posterity happens to come upon them,

> the rare Characters who may read and be pleased with them, will be looked upon as singular and whimsical, as in these days an Admirer of Suarez, Aquinas or Dionysius Areopagita.[9]

As for the *Speculum humanae salvationis*, even before Stiles read it through and discovered its presentation of the doctrine of St. Thomas Aquinas, he must have been attracted to the work by the "Prohemium." In this preface the author states that he has prepared his book for the instruction of the many on the supreme matter of man's salvation. Since the learned can read the Scriptures, the *Speculum*, he writes, will present for the untutored only the material relevant to the Creation, the Fall, and the Redemption, all rendered comprehensible through pictures. He then adds a parable to show that his book may be of use to a wide variety of persons. Once in a certain abbey, a great oak had to be cut down, yet every bit of the fallen tree was put to use by the members of the community: the trunk for an anvil for the smith, the bark for the shoemaker for tanning leather, the timber for the carpenter, the curved branches for the fisherman's boat, the galls for ink for the scribe, etc. So the writer hopes that his interpretation of the essence of Holy Scripture will serve diverse people for their special benefit. Confronted with such a challenge, Ezra Stiles, the "Gentle Puritan," must gladly have accepted the invitation of this wise disciple of the "Angelic Doctor," St. Thomas Aquinas.

TWO POEMS FROM A FORGED MANUSCRIPT. *Left: Elegy* of Tyrtaeus in boustrophedon. *Right: The Axe* of Simmias, figure poem

Beinecke Rare Book and Manuscript Library, Yale University, MS 580

A Forged Manuscript
in Boustrophedon

THAT SUPERLATIVE ACHIEVEMENT of Western man, the invention of the Greek alphabet, was variously credited to the Three Fates, to Mercury, to the semi-mythical King Cadmus, and, finally, to the ingenious Greek hero Palamedes. Legend finds the origin of Palamedes' discovery in his observation of a natural phenomenon, the migratory flight of the cranes. When the Greeks took from the Phoenicians their "retrograde" method of writing, that is, from right to left, they soon altered it to a scheme of their own. They started from the right with the letters reversed, then at the extreme left turned and continued to the right with the letters in the familiar form, turning again at the extreme right with reversed letters, and so on. Like Palamedes, they found a parallel for this invention also in the world of nature, for they thought it resembled oxen plowing a field, going first in one direction and then turning and continuing in the opposite. It was for this reason that they called the writing "boustrophedon," that is, "ox-turning."

By the fifth century this system of writing had been replaced entirely by the simpler left-to-right pattern that has prevailed ever since, but there remain a considerable number of fragmentary inscriptions on durable materials in the boustrophedon style. Of these, the so-called Sigeian inscription, now in the British Library, is the best known. Carved on the base of a marble funeral monument from Sigeum and belonging to the early sixth century, it has two texts, one in the Attic dialect and the other in the Ionic.[1] In literature, references to this type of writing include Plutarch's statement (*Solon*, 25) that the laws of Solon were written in the ancient style, but in his time only a few relics of the original wooden tablets remained in the Prytaneum in Athens. Pausanias, making a tour of Greece in the second century of our era, describes an elaborate chest, a votive offering at the temple of Hera at Olympia to commemorate the preservation of Cypselus, later tyrant of Corinth, when as an infant he was hidden away from the hostile Bacchiadeae. In addition to the gold and ivory and beautiful carvings of scenes from mythology, Pausanias notes, that

> ... on the chest there are inscriptions in large letters in an old handwriting, some of the writing is straight, other parts are written in what the Greeks call "ox-fashion." That is, when one line is finished the next begins where that left off and runs backward, and so on, like the double course of the raceground. (*Description of Greece*, V.17.5)

Any early literary works that may have been written in boustrophedon were less fortunate than the inscriptions and none has survived. Written on fragile papyrus, without the protection of covers, in times of violent political changes, many had been lost long before the Alexandrian period when scholars were making a great effort to collect and preserve the older literature of Greece. As it happens, some of these writings were saved in parts only because they were imbedded in works of later writers. In this way, for example, the longest fragment of the

Exhortations of Tyrtaeus, the Greek elegiac poet who lived in Sparta about the middle of the seventh century B.C., was preserved through its quotation by the Attic orator Lycurgus in his speech "Against Leochares."

In view of these facts, then, it is surprising to find in the Beinecke Library a vellum manuscript (MS. 580) which not only gives the text of four of Tyrtaeus' poems, but has it written in boustrophedon. The manuscript consists of two small scrolls of fine vellum, measuring 480 by 55 millimeters, written in brown ink in Greek capitals. One scroll contains elegies of Tyrtaeus, the other the figure- or pattern-poems (which the Greeks called *technopaignia*) of the Hellenistic poets Dosiadas of Crete, Simmias of Rhodes, Theocritus, and Besantinus. These poems were so arranged that the position of the lines formed the shape of the object named in the title of the poem.[2]

This miniature manuscript, purported to have been written in Greece in the third century, belonged to the library of the great English collector Sir Thomas Phillipps, where it was numbered 13881. Knowledge of the circumstances under which the manuscript was acquired by Sir Thomas for his collection may help to evaluate the significance of the texts preserved in it.[3] In his limitless zeal for adding to his vast holdings in books and manuscripts, Sir Thomas sometimes explored unusual and even dubious sources of supply, and our manuscript falls into the latter category. In 1853 there arrived in London a Greek scholar, Constantine Simonides, with a large number of Greek manuscripts, many by classical authors, which he offered for sale to the British Museum. Sir Frederic Madden, Keeper of Manuscripts, not only denounced Simonides' manuscripts as forgeries but warned the librarian of the Bodleian Library to be on the alert for the impostor. When, however, Sir Thomas Phillipps heard of the remarkable Greek visitor and his hoard of manuscripts, purported to come from Mount Athos, he invited Simonides to visit him at Middle Hill and to bring his manuscripts. The Greek accepted the invitation, but brought only a small number of his

choicest items. Sir Thomas was instantly enthralled by a miniature vellum scroll of Hesiod, written in boustrophedon, and
bought it immediately.

During the next ten years and repeated visits, Simonides sold
twenty-two manuscripts, some forgeries, some authentic, to Sir
Thomas. Of these, several miniature scrolls held a particular
fascination for the collector: (1) the *Carmina* of Anacreon on four
rolls of the thinnest imaginable vellum, measuring less than an
inch in width and seven inches in length, with letters so small
that it was almost impossible to read them even with the aid of a
magnifying glass; (2) the *Aurea carmina* of Pythagoras on one
roll, written in letters almost as small as those in the Anacreon;
(3) the *Elegies* of Tyrtaeus, written in boustrophedon, with
several figure-poems of Dosiadas, Simmias, Theocritus, and
Besantinus; (4) the *Poema* attributed to Phocylides, with a poem
of Rhianus and Aristotle's "Hymn to Virtue" on seven rolls of
vellum; and (5)—the greatest treasure of all—three books of the
Iliad on a long vellum roll written in almost microscopic letters,
in boustrophedon style.[4] Although the paleographers of the
British Museum and the Bodleian Library warned him that
Simonides was a notorious forger and that these manuscripts
were the products of his unquestioned calligraphic skill,
Phillipps still maintained his belief in their authenticity and only
very reluctantly in later years conceded that the Tyrtaeus and the
Phocylides might possibly be spurious because they were written
in larger capitals and in brown ink.

When the great library at Middle Hill was dispersed, the
manuscripts found their way into widely scattered repositories.
Some of the last to be auctioned were the miniature vellum
scrolls, and three of these, the Anacreon along with the
Pythagoras, the Tyrtaeus, and the Pseudo–Phocylides, were
bought by Hans P. Kraus, who, with Mrs. Kraus, presented
them to Yale as rare examples of the work of "one of the most
celebrated and learned of all forgers, Constantine Simonides."[5]

Of the three manuscripts, the Anacreon is more interesting as
a literary curiosity than useful as a text because it is almost

impossible to read the tiny faded letters. Sir Thomas boasted that the whole manuscript, if folded, would easily fit into a walnut shell.[6] The text attributed to Phocylides, the writer of epigrams in the sixth century, is actually a moral poem, *Poema Nutheticum*, by a Jewish writer of the second century B.C. By contrast, the Tyrtaeus manuscript contains an authentic text, the script is large enough to be read, and it is a fine piece of calligraphy.

The Tyrtaeus manuscript has several noteworthy physical features. In the first place, it consists of two long, narrow strips of thin vellum with writing on both sides, rolled tightly into a scroll, though as a general rule vellum was not used for manuscripts until the fourth century of our era. One of the strips contains four elegies of Tyrtaeus written in one continuous column the length of the strip and extending halfway down the *verso*. Normally, comparable texts written on papyrus were arranged in short, relatively narrow columns so that the scroll could be rolled up on the left as it was unrolled on the right. Further, it is written in beautiful capital letters commonly used in inscriptions, while the script used for papyrus was less formal and closer to cursive. Still more unusual, it is written in boustrophedon style, although by the fifth century this method had long been superseded by the simpler left-to-right system, as Herodotus (*History*, II.36) testifies. Finally, for the poems of Tyrtaeus there was no continuous manuscript tradition. In the first half of the seventh century when the patriot Tyrtaeus was trying to rally the Spartans in their desperate struggle for survival, his *Marching Songs* and *Exhortations* were effective in unifying and thus saving the state. The spirited songs were admired and sung on countless other occasions, but there is no evidence that they were written down or that any edition was made until Alexandrian times. By then only fragments were still in existence and modern editors depend for texts upon these late collections and quotations in other Greek writers.

The first scroll of this unconventional manuscript contains four elegies of Tyrtaeus, exhorting the Spartans to valor to retrieve their ancestral reputation for courage.[7] These verses, all

in boustrophedon, amount to a hundred lines (not verses) on the
recto and fifty-four lines on the *verso* of the narrow scroll. Halfway down the *verso* the first of a series of figure-poems[8]
occurs—the "Altar" of Dosiadas, written in various meters, with
the lines shaping an altar. This very difficult and tortured poem,
laden with mythological references, seems to convey the simple
message that it was erected by Jason rather than by Achilles.
Simonides, however, was not content to copy the poem line-by-
line as it appears in the unique *Palatine Anthology* manuscript and
in the printed copies taken from it, but rather he chose to make a
very complicated, intricate version of his own. First he arranged
single letters in nine vertical parallel columns, beginning at the
left and extending down four letters. Beneath that he made four
lines in boustrophedon to form the upper part of the altar. These
were followed by eight vertical rows of single letters beginning
at the right. The base of the altar had two lines in boustrophedon, then two lines crossing at acute angles, and a final single line.

The second scroll begins with another figure-poem, also an
"Altar," that of the obscure poet Besantinus. Speaking in the
first person, the altar says that it was erected by the Muses and it
invites offerings of Hymettan honey. The original poem is
acrostic, but Simonides made of this, too, an elaborate structure
of vertical lines of single letters alternating with three sections in
boustrophedon writing. There follow two more figure-poems of
Simmias, known as the "Wings" and the "Axe." The first,
which represents the wings of Love, is spoken by the ancient
divinity Eros, who rules the universe by gentle persuasion. In
the manuscript the wings are formed simply by six lines of words
reading from right to left, with a matching set of lines reading
from left to right. The "Axe" is the double-edged weapon of
Epeus (who built the wooden horse) and is the instrument by
which the walls of Troy were torn down. In the manuscript the
figure is achieved by six vertical parallel lines of letters in their
normal formation, then a single vertical line of letters extending
from the center to another set of six vertical lines of reversed
letters.

The *verso* of the second scroll contains another figure-poem of Simmias, the "Egg." This tells the story of the egg that was stolen by Mercury from the nest of a nightingale in order that he might give the rules of poetry and song to men. Less intricately contrived than the other figures, the great egg is formed by a series of ever-increasing lines, followed by a set of similar decreasing ones. After this there occurs an ingenious but puzzling poem attributed to Theocritus and called "Pan's Pipe." It is made in the shape of a shepherd's syrinx and was supposed to have been inscribed on the uneven reeds of the instrument. Except that it is written in boustrophedon, the figure of twenty lines, each one shorter than the preceding to represent the reeds, is much like the original in the *Palatine Anthology*.

Two more little-known poems, both also from the *Palatine Anthology*,[9] complete the texts on the *verso* of the second scroll and occupy forty-two lines. They are not figure-poems, but are written in boustrophedon. The first, "Hymn to Nemesis," was the work of a minor poet Mesomedes, a native of Crete and a freedman of the emperor Hadrian. Here the poet addresses Nemesis, not as the primitive goddess who punishes insolent behavior, but rather as the goddess of fate who deals out to men their lot in life. The daughter of Justice, she seems akin to the divinity whom the Romans called Fortuna. The second poem, a "Hymn to Poseidon," is traditionally attributed to Arion, the early Greek poet who was considered the inventor of the dithyramb. In view of Herodotus' well-known story (*Hist.*, I.23) of Arion and the dolphin who saved his life, it seems appropriate that the poem is a hymn to Poseidon. In it the poet recalls his dramatic rescue to Taenarum as he gives full credit to the greatest of the gods, the ruler of the seas.

The small manuscript, then, contains a most unusual combination of texts, from the seventh-century elegies of Tyrtaeus to the poem of Mesomedes of the second century of our era. Further, in spirit, they range from the patriotic exhortations of Tyrtaeus to the sophisticated hymn to Nemesis. In form, too, they show wide variation from the puzzling figure-poem attributed to Theocritus to the hymn to Poseidon, made noteworthy by being written in boustrophedon.

Now, to return to the legend of that brilliant genius Palamedes, who invented the Greek alphabet, it is recorded that, near the end of the Trojan War, he was tricked and put to death through a ruse which was possible only because, among the unlettered Greeks, he was known to have the rare accomplishment of being able to read and write. It is said that Odysseus, to avenge a long-standing grudge, had placed in Palamedes' tent a sack of gold along with a forged letter from King Priam, arranging for him to betray the Greeks. In this tale perhaps there is a rough parallel, though in reverse, to the case of Simonides, who also became the victim of his own specialized knowledge. If he had been less learned in paleography and less skillful in calligraphy, perhaps he would have restricted his activities to copying more ordinary texts and in the conventional way, and his forgeries might have gone undetected at least for a longer time. As it happened, his studies took him into ancient Greek inscriptions, and he became so fascinated with boustrophedon writing that it served as a challenge to his skill. This may explain his strange lack of caution when he copied in boustrophedon literary works that were first created long after the ancient method of writing had been forgotten. Even more remarkable was Simonides' obsession with the Hellenistic figure-poems. Apparently the poets' achievements in accommodating substance and meter to such strict limits of form served to stimulate his imagination. With the greatest ingenuity, while keeping the prescribed shape, though different from the original, Simonides completely rearranged the letters into intricate patterns, thus creating a puzzle that would test the wits of any reader. One might almost conclude that Constantine Simonides was inviting detection of his fraud in order to win admiration for his cleverness.

RENAISSANCE LEARNING

Theophilacti scolasti‑
ci Simocati eple morales:rurales
et amatorie interpretatione latina.

FACSIMILE COPY OF TITLE PAGE OF COPERNICUS' LATIN TRANSLATION OF
THEOPHYLACTUS SIMOCATTA'S *Epistles*, Cracow, 1509

Sterling Memorial Library, Yale University

Copernicus' Stand
for Humanism

IN 1509, WHEN NICHOLAS COPERNICUS, canon of Frauenberg, returned to Cracow on a political mission with his uncle, Bishop Wacsenrode of Ermland, he took the opportunity to ask his old acquaintance, the bookseller and printer, Johannes Haller, to publish a book of his. Earlier, Copernicus had spent four years (1492–1495) at the University of Cracow where he was enrolled in courses in the Faculty of the Arts, but he also attended lectures on mathematics and astronomy. To complete his education, he then spent eight years in Italy, interrupted by two journeys back to Poland. In Bologna for three and a half years he studied canon law in preparation for a career in the Church, but he also took time to pursue his interest in astronomy with a renowned scientist, Domenico Maria Novara. During these years he also learned Greek. For the Jubilee Year of 1500, he was in Rome where he was invited to give lectures on mathematics and astronomy at the University. From there he went to Padua, to complete his studies in law, though eventually he took his

degree of Doctor of Canon Law at the University of Ferrara in
1503. Back in Padua, he entered the School of Medicine and
studied for two years before he was called home to Poland to
assume the duties of physician to his uncle, the bishop.
Copernicus returned intellectually enriched by his formal studies
and by his wide reading in classical literature and philosophy, as
well as by his association with some of the leaders of the
humanist movement in Italy.

While he was attending his uncle, Copernicus visited Cracow
and took with him the manuscript of a book which was to
identify him as a humanist and to mark the publisher as one of
the first to print humanist literature in Poland. Copernicus' book,
*Theophilacti Scholastici Simocati Epistole morales, rurales, et ama-
toriae, interpretatione latina*, was his Latin translation of eighty-five
epistles composed by the seventh-century Byzantine historian,
Theophylactus Simocatta.[1] The *Epistles* are divided into groups,
each of which contains a moral, a rural, and an amatory letter.
These imaginary epistles must have been composed as a kind of
literary diversion for the author who represents them as letters
between historical persons or characters in literary works. It is
not known when or where Copernicus first came upon this little
book, nor is it clear why he took such pains with a subject so far
removed from his scientific interests. Ironically, it was the only
one of his books that he had the satisfaction of seeing in print.

Johannes Haller published Copernicus' translation in a fine
little volume.[2] Copies of this original are now exceedingly rare,[3]
but recently a Polish scholar has had a facsimile printed along
with the Greek text and a modern edition of the translation.[4]
Copernicus' name does not appear on the original title page,
which is nonetheless a very striking one. Below the three-line
title, the whole page is taken up with a splendid woodcut
divided into two levels. On the upper half, a large lion and a fine
unicorn are supporting a shield upon which are emblazoned the
arms of Poland, an eagle with wings outstretched and wearing a
crown with three crosses. Below this, two shields are depicted;
on the left is a shield with the arms of Cracow, a great city-wall

with large gates, open, and surmounted by three towers. The other shield has the arms of the Jagello kings of Poland, a warrior in full armour on a spirited horse, charging with an upraised lance, and holding a shield with a cross with double arms. Between the two shields the printer's device with Haller's initials occupies a conspicuous position.

The small volume consists of forty-one unnumbered pages printed in a bold Gothic type, with large chapter heads and very elaborate decorative initials. The text of Copernicus' translation is preceded by a long introductory poem in elegiac couplets composed by his friend, Laurentius Corvinus, who was at that time serving as town clerk of Breslau in Silesia. This scholar had had a varied career. He had written a manual of geography, *Cosmographia*, published in Basel in 1496, and taught at the University of Cracow when Copernicus was a student there. Corvinus' poem offers a warm welcome to one who has long been in Italy, upon his return to his home in northern lands that lie close under the constellations of the two Bears and of Boötes. It is full of echoes of Virgil's *Georgics*, as he sings the praises of his own beautiful country. He pays graceful tribute to Sigismund I, King of Poland (lines 37–40), and to Hedwigis, Duchess of Silesia (81–1). He speaks of Bishop Wacsenrode as the Aeneas for whom Copernicus was the faithful Achates (25). The most notable lines of the poem (27–31) are those in which he characterizes Copernicus as one who "traces the swift course of the moon and the alternating journeys of her brother and the wandering planets, the marvellous work of the Almighty, and who knows how to discover the hidden causes from these wonderful beginnings."

Copernicus' short prose dedication to his uncle constitutes his justification for making the translation of Theophylactus' *Epistles*. He explains the inclusion of a variety of types—moral, rural, and amatory—as recognition of the fact that men's tastes differ, so some will appeal to one person, some to another. He describes the little book as a garden full of flowers, from which one may select those that appeal to him, and admits that while

some of the epistles are frivolous, they are not immoral; indeed
they might all be called moral. He then speaks of his great debt
to his uncle as he offers this small gift in gratitude to him.

Copernicus made a faithful, almost literal, translation of the
eighty-five Greek epistles of Theophylactus, yet with a real
feeling for style. The imaginary writers fall into a wide range of
categories. There are, for example, four written by different
Muses. A larger number are written by mythological characters,
of whom the most famous are Medea, Atalanta, Leander,
Eurydice, Galatea, and Chryses. The majority are reputed to
have been written by historical personages. Of these the philosophers are prominent: Socrates, Plato, Chrysippus, Antisthenes,
Parmenides, Aristoxenus, and Plotinus. There are also a number
of political figures: Pericles, Critias, Alcibiades, Themistocles,
and Aeschines. Another group was written by poets: Terpander,
Sosipater, Telesilla, Corinna, and Moschion. Appropriately, the
senders and recipients of the rural epistles are such "characters"
as Poplar Tree (Aigirus), Plane Tree (Platanus), Laurel Grove
(Daphnon), Grapevine (Ampelinum), Garden Herbs (Lachanon),
Rose (Rodon), Gazelle (Dorcon), and Cicada (Tettigon).

All of these epistles are quite simple, each bearing a single
message. A "moral" letter from Socrates to Plato (40), for
instance, begins with the familiar thesis: "No one is injured by a
wrong done to him, but the one who inflicts the wrong only
injures himself." After giving several illustrations, he concludes,
"I have always admired the Cyclops in Homer, for he says that
no man can harm one who endures an injury, and that "the
negation of the shepherd is the affirmation of truth." Another
"moral" epistle in a different tone is one by Plato to Axiochus
(70), where the writer observes, "We control horses by means of
reins but also by whips; we keep ships on course sometimes by
spreading their sails and again by restraining them with anchors.
So, Axiochus, the tongue must be controlled, sometimes by
arming it with words, but again by forcing it into silence." In
another (82), Socrates, writing to Alcibiades, reminds him that
there is a great deal of wisdom in poetry. He recalls Homer's

account of Odysseus and the songs of the Sirens, which should teach that only when one binds himself by the chains of philosophy can he withstand the temptations of pleasure.

In one of the "amatory" epistles (42), Pericles says to Aspasia, "If you expect gifts from me, you do not love me, for love cannot be bought with gifts. If, then, you love, it is appropriate that you give, rather than receive." In another (15), the girl athlete, Atalanta, who has had only contempt for her suitors, confesses to Corinna that she has just seen Augias in the palestra and that she has fallen in love with him. Leander, in another epistle (45), writes to Pylades that he is in love, but that the lady of his choice hates him. He blames the Amores for this unjust situation and challenges them to change their ways.

The "rural" epistles are simple messages concerning matters of interest in farm and animal husbandry. Anthinus, for example (83), reminds Ampelinus that the grape harvest is at hand and advises him to look out for wayfarers and to discourage them from ravaging the fruit by keeping a large dog in the vineyard. In another, (68), Seutlion tells Coriannus that he has caught a little fox that has been causing great damage and he thinks he should call in the neighbors and make a public exhibition of his punishment of the offender. Again (23), Astachion writes to Milon telling him to rid his field of hemlock for it is destroying his bees. If he does not comply, Astachion will inscribe the injustice on his doors and let all the neighbors know of it.

The significance of this slim volume of epistles translated by Copernicus is not to be measured by their slight literary or philosophical importance, but rather by the fact that the book publicly enrolled the translator as a sympathizer with the new humanist movement that seemed a threat to the old conservative scholastic philosophy which had dominated Poland for so long. The book carried a certain defence against criticism in the fact that it was dedicated to Bishop Wacsenrode, one of the most influential of the Polish prelates. Even with this *imprimatur*, however, the publication of a Greek book was so far from being welcomed that it was generally ignored. This may be explained

by the bitterness of the scholastic-humanistic confrontation in
northern Europe which is evidenced by the fact that at the very
time of the publication of Copernicus' translation in Cracow, the
greatest of the German humanists, Johann Reuchlin, was suffer-
ing persecution because of his unorthodox activities of teaching
Greek and Hebrew. Although Copernicus spent the rest of his
life largely on the study of mathematics and astronomy, he did
write another small literary work which would identify him as
being in the humanist tradition. It is the Latin translation
of a letter supposedly written by the Pythagorean Lysis to
Hipparchus, also a pupil of Pythagoras, advising him of the
necessity for keeping the tenets of their philosophy within the
society to avoid misinterpretation by the uneducated. Copernicus
cites this letter in the dedication to Pope Paul III of his *De
revolutionibus* and originally added the whole translation to the
end of Book I, though he deleted it before the book was
published in 1543.[5] A third literary work long attributed to him
has now been discredited. It is a Greek epigram composed as an
introduction to the long Latin epithalamium written by Joannes
Dantiscus[6] for the wedding of King Sigismund I to Barbara
Zanolya in 1512. Further evidence for Copernicus' interest in
humanism is seen in a list of books in his library.[7]

Quite apart from its place in the life of Copernicus, the
publication of his translation of Theophylactus Simocatta's
Epistles in 1509 had greater significance in the cultural history of
Poland. It was the first printing of a Greek author in that
country. This was eleven years before Greek was taught at the
University of Cracow. Officially the state still resisted the introduction of humanist writings into Poland, but the intellectual
atmosphere of the new movement had been gradually filtering
into the country since the generation before Copernicus' time.[8]
Never insulated against scholars from the north, particularly
Holland and Germany, and from Italy, the educated Poles had
met such learned men as Conrad Celtes, the renowned classicist,
who stayed in Poland for two years (1487–1489) and founded a
literary society (Sodalitas litteraria Vistulana) which attracted the

foremost intellectuals of that day. In a similar way, an Italian expatriate who called himself Callimachus (Felippo Buonacorsi) spent over twenty-five years (1470–1496) in Cracow, at times lecturing at the Academy and always taking a prominent role in the activities of the literary society. Besides keeping in touch with leaders of the Renaissance in Italy and communicating news of the humanist trends developing in that country, he undertook diplomatic missions for the king, and even found time to write poetry. He also wrote a biography of his friend, the Polish scholar, Gregory of Sanok, who, like Callimachus, was one of the most influential of the precursors of humanism. After years of wandering in Germany and in Italy, he returned to take his place as one of the leaders of the scholars of his own country. His great collection of books and his lectures on classical texts served to stimulate interest in the new attitude toward life that was beginning to be felt in Poland.

Since the intellectual circles in Poland had thus long been fired with enthusiasm for the new ideas on the values of life and the nature of man, as they listened to the foreign scholars and to their own who had returned from their studies abroad, and brought back books to illuminate their new philosophy, clearly the time had come for some overt act of public recognition of the values of humanistic philosophy. So it was that when the young Copernicus, encouraged by his old friend, Corvinus, a member of the literary society, published his Latin translation of the Greek *Epistles* of Theophylactus Simocatta, he openly took his stand for humanism. Even though the book remained in obscurity for a decade, nevertheless it had quietly served as a catalytic agent which eventually transformed Poland into a Renaissance society. By a happy chance, Copernicus himself, toward the end of his life, characterized the new humanistic attitude toward learning. In the Introduction to his great *De revolutionibus*, in words more commonly associated with a poet than a scientist, he composed a kind of apologia for his life-time study of astronomy. In the first paragraph he gives his reasons for considering astronomy the queen of the sciences. He says,

"Of the many and diverse sciences and arts by which the human spirit is quickened, in my opinion, those which are concerned with the most beautiful subjects and are most worthy of being studied should be cultivated most earnestly and pursued with the greatest zeal. Such is that science that deals with the marvellous movements in the universe, with the courses of the planets, their size, distances, risings and settings, and the causes of other celestial phenomena which explain the whole structure of the universe. For what is more beautiful than the heavens which, indeed, comprise all beauty? This is indicated by the very names "caelum" and "mundus"; by the word "mundus" their purity and beauty are designated, by "caelum", their sublimity. Because of their consummate grandeur, by many philosophers the heavens have been called the visible god."[9]

A Roman Proverb

in Sixteenth-Century England

AULUS GELLIUS, A LATIN WRITER of the second century A.D., is
the source of our information about the origin of a Roman
proverb which had a special appeal for the sixteenth century in
England. In his *Attic Nights* (*Noctes Atticae*), a large collection
of essays on historical, philological, and philosophical topics, he
gives two versions of the text. He says that as a schoolboy he
heard a quotation from the Roman Stoic philosopher, Musonius
Rufus, that seemed such a brilliant and true sentiment that he
committed it to memory.[1] He then gives the Greek text, which
can be translated:

> If you accomplish something noble though with toil, the toil
> passes, but the noble deed remains; if you do something
> dishonorable with pleasure, the pleasure passes, but the
> dishonor remains.

Musonius Rufus lived in the first century and taught philosophy
in Rome. Associated with the political victims of Nero, he was

exiled by that emperor, and again, under Vespasian, he was banished along with other philosophers. Like Socrates, Musonius made no attempt to preserve his discourses on philosophy, but some of his writings have survived because they were collected in the anthology of Stobaeus in the fifth century.[2] For the quotation under consideration, however, Aulus Gellius is the sole source.[3]

In his discussion of the proverb, Aulus Gellius remarks that later he came upon the same sentiment in a speech of Marcus Cato *To the Knights at Numantia*, which he delivered in 195 B.C. Although he finds it less concise and less aptly expressed, he quotes it since it is earlier than Musonius' words and worthy of respect because of its antiquity. Translated from the Latin, it reads:

> Consider this in your hearts: if you accomplish some good attended with toil, the toil will quickly leave you, but the good that you gained will never depart from you; but if you do some evil attended with pleasure, the pleasure will quickly pass away, but the evil will remain with you forever.[4]

Cato, the rugged statesman, warrior, and stern reformer, whose literary works were on history and agriculture, may have been expressing a sentiment that had been passed down in oral tradition from long before his time. It would not be surprising if the proverb was derived from a Greek source, but Aulus Gellius, who was a Hellenophile and lived for a time in Athens, makes no suggestion of a Greek origin. It was not until the nineteenth century that an English scholar[5] pointed out a comparable sentiment in a work of the fifth-century Greek orator, Isocrates.[6] Since, however, this version differs significantly and seems not to have come to the attention of any of the writers with whom we are concerned, I shall not consider it here.

In later Latin literature, strangely enough, the proverb, neither as given by Cato nor in the wording of Musonius Rufus, was repeated.[7] Only in the fifth century, the Neoplatonic philosopher, Hierocles of Alexandria, in his Greek *Commentary on the*

Golden Verses of Pythagoras, used Musonius' quotation, though without acknowledgment. Elaborating the aphorism that the happy life can result only from virtuous acts, he says, reversing the sequence of ideas:

> If something shameful is done with pleasure, the pleasure passes, but the shame remains; if, however, something honorable is done with toil, the toil passes, but the honorable deed remains.[8]

It was not until the sixteenth century that the old Roman proverb was quoted as applying to contemporary society. Of those who adopted the sentiment as their own, I should like to consider two people of prominence, Princess Mary, later Queen of Scots, and Sir Humphrey Gilbert.

Sometime before 1558, Mary presented to one of her ladies-in-waiting a beautiful Book of Hours in which she inscribed an unusual dedication. This book is now in the Bodleian Library[9] to which it had been given in 1615 after Henry's death by the solicitor of Prince Henry. The inscription, at the beginning of the Psalms, has been badly rubbed but is still legible. It reads:

> Geate you such riches as when the shype is broken, may swyme away wythe the Master. For dyverse chances take away the goods of fortune; but the goods of the soule whych bee only the trewe goods, nother fyer not water can take away. Yf you take labour and payne to doo a vertuous thyng, the labour goeth away, and the vertue remaynethe, Yf through pleasure you do any vicious thyng, the pleasure goeth away and the vice remaynethe. Good Madam, for my sake, remembre thys.

> Your lovyng mystress, Marye Princesse

The first and second sentences with their apt metaphor follow the general pattern of sentiments considered appropriate for a religious book. The third and fourth sentences are the old Roman proverb as given by Musonius Rufus. Where did Mary find the quotation? She could not have seen it in any edition of Aulus Gellius. The *editio princeps* of the *Noctes Atticae* was made in Rome in 1467, and it was printed by Aldus in Venice in 1515, but it was not printed in northern Europe until 1706 when J.F. and G. Gronov published it in Leyden. No English translation appeared until 1795, when W. Beloe printed it in London.

Mary was quite young when she wrote the inscription, and was still being taught by eminent tutors in English, French, and Latin, as well as in Italian and Spanish, so one might hope to find a clue in other writings of hers that have survived. There is a series of sixty-four Latin compositions, dated 1554, which she translated from the French originals provided by one of her instructors.[10] In Mary's Latin version many of them are put into the form of letters to one or another of her friends. A great many are discussions of the virtues as the basis for the good life; they cite Plato, Plutarch, Cicero, Socrates, and Solomon, as well as Aesop, Cato, and even Erasmus. Fifteen of these letters are concerned with citations of learned women, Biblical, mythological, Greek, Roman, and even a few contemporaries. There is no reference to the proverb under discussion. Neither does a list, made in 1578, of one hundred and fifty books in the Queen's library, provide a clue to the provenance of the quotation.[11] Here are books in English, French, and Latin, with a few in Italian. They include history, biography, also the Bible and devotional works, poetry, medieval romance, and books on sports. Since the list is prefaced by the warning that it represents only the "Books saved from the general wreck of what had been the Royal Library of Scotland in the reign of Queen Mary," one is free to speculate on what other books it once contained where the proverb might have been given. Perhaps it included some of the florilegia, books on the virtues and the vices, memorable sayings of the philosophers, and comonplace books that were so highly prized in the sixteenth century.

It is interesting to note that, some thirty-five years after the young Princess Mary inscribed the Musonius proverb in English in a Book of Hours, her son, James VI of Scotland (later James I of England), as a young boy copied the same proverb, though in Latin, in two different places in a small volume now in the

British Library (Add. 34275) and signed his name "Jacobus
R."[12] The paper manuscript of only twenty folios, bound in
limp vellum, contains a rough catalogue of some of the books in
the Royal Library of Scotland and was written by Peter Young,
one of James's tutors. The inscriptions seem to represent casual
practice exercises with no relevance to the contents of the
volume. Possibly James was practicing in order to make a fair
copy for some more important place.[13]

If, in the sixteenth century, the Roman proverb was considered appropriate for the moral educational training of young
royalty, it was by no means restricted to that area of social life.
As evidence of this, one may cite an example of its use in the
writings of Sir Humphrey Gilbert, who is credited with planting
the first British colony in America. This distinguished navigator,
who was educated at Eton and Oxford and was widely read in
philosophy, quotes the proverb at the end of his famous *Discourse
of a Discoverie for a New Passage to Cataia.*[14] Written in 1576 to
persuade Queen Elizabeth to sponsor an expedition to find a
northwest passage to China and the East Indies, the treatise
exhibits great learning, as Gilbert produces an abundance of
testimonia ranging from Plato's account of the lost island of
Atlantis and quotations from Aristotle and Strabo's *Geography*, to
a comprehensive listing of quotations from contemporary geo-
graphers and navigators from Italy, Spain, the Netherlands,
Germany, France, and England, to support his contention that
the bold enterprise he proposed was not only feasible but certain
to be of great advantage to England. He concludes with a
personal appeal to the Queen, vowing the commitment of his
life to his country:

> Desiring you hereafter never to mistake with me, for the
> taking in hand of any laudable and honest enterprise; for if
> through pleasure or idlenes we purchase shame, ye pleasure
> vanisheth, but the shame remaineth forever.[15]

Here one has the second half of the Roman proverb translated
quite freely, in the version of Cato rather than of Musonius

The Table.

the ſhoꝛtening of any diſcouerie, to know
at the firſt entring of any fret, whether it
lye open to the Ocean, moꝛe wayes then
one, how farre ſoeuer the ſea ſtretcheth it
ſelfe, into the land.

Deſiring you hereafter, neu er to miſ-
like with me, foꝛ the taking in hand of a-
ny laudable and honeſt enterpꝛiſe, foꝛ if
thꝛough pleaſure oꝛ idlenes we purchaſe
ſhame, ÿ pleaſure baniſheth, but the ſhame
remaineth foꝛ euer.

And therefoꝛe to giue me leaue without offence, alwayes to liue and die in this
minde, That he is not vvorthie to liue at all,
that for feare, or daunger of death, shunneth his
countrey ſeruice, and his ovvne honour·
ſeeing death is ineuitable, and the
fame of bertue immoꝛtall.
Wherfoꝛe in this behalfe,
Mutare vel timere
ſperno.

*Feriæ qui vm-
bras timet.*

FINIS.

SIR HUMPHREY GILBERT'S CITATION OF A ROMAN PROVERB. *Discourse of a*
Discoverie for a New Passage to Cataia (London, 1576) final page.

Beinecke Rare Book and Manuscript Library, Yale University

Rufus.[16] The most obvious source of the quotation and the one most accessible to English scholars must have been *De vita et moribus philosophorum* [*Lives and characters of the philosophers*] written by the English Franciscan, Walter Burley, in the early fourteenth century. The large volume contains the lives and teachings of one hundred and thirty-two Greek and Roman philosophers, historians, statesmen, and poets, largely derived from Diogenes Laertius. Over one hundred and fifty manuscripts of this work are still extant [17] and there were thirty editions printed before 1530, as well as translations into Spanish, Italian, German, and Polish before 1500. No English translation was made. Cato the Elder was one of the Roman statesmen whose life Burley included. After outlining Cato's accomplishments in war and in government, he cites the speech delivered at Numantia, and gives the proverb.[18] Except for a few minor differences in word order, it is the same as the Aulus Gellius citation. This would seem a reasonable source for Sir Humphrey Gilbert's one quotation.

For an example of the application to contemporary society of the Roman proverb as it occurs in the third version, that is, in the words of Hierocles in his *Commentary on the Golden Verses of Pythagoras*, one must go beyond the sixteenth century to 1633, when a collection of the poems of George Herbert was published shortly after the poet's death. The son of a prominent Welsh family, Herbert was educated first by tutors, then at Westminster School and Cambridge where, after taking his degree, he was reader in rhetoric and then orator for the University. The political changes occasioned by the death of James I in 1625 and his own growing conviction of a religious vocation led him to become an Anglican priest. Throughout his life Herbert had been writing religious poetry, but he had published none of it. Before his death he gave permission to a friend to publish his great collection of poems, *The Temple*, in which he commemorates every aspect of the Church of England and reveals his own joy at the privilege of serving it as priest. In this collection *The Church Porch* is concluded with the couplet from Hierocles:

If thou do ill, the joy fades, not the pains;
If well, the pain doth fade, the joy remains.[19]

Herbert, though widely read in contemporary as well as in classical literature, left few clues as to the source of his references, so it is hard to conjecture where he came upon the Hierocles quotation. The *Commentary* was copied in at least twenty-seven manuscripts from the tenth century to the fifteenth and portions of it were copied in conjunction with a number of other similar works.[20] The first Latin translation was made in Padua in 1450 by Giovanni Aurispa, and the Greek *editio princeps* was printed in Paris in 1583 by Joannes Cuterius. No English translation of Hierocles was made until that of John Hall published in London in 1651. Books of quotations and collections of memorable sayings, so popular in the sixteenth century, would seem to be more likely sources for Herbert's quotation from Hierocles than any of the complete editions of his works.

If one were to draw any conclusion after observing the tradition of the old Roman proverb from the second century B.C. down through the sixteenth century, it must be that the epigram not only had great vitality but that it was universally accepted as true. The pragmatist, farmer, soldier and statesman, Cato, found it valid; the gentle Stoic philosopher, Musonius, who had endured more evils than a man might reasonably expect, felt it was necessary to repeat the advice to his disciples; the idealistic scholar, Hierocles, in expounding the best of the sayings of Pythagoras, considered the sentiment in harmony with the theme of one of the *Golden Verses*. None of these writers claimed credit for the memorable saying and none gave any hint of its origin. Like Aulus Gellius, who as a schoolboy memorized it because it was not only striking, but true, the ancient scholars accepted it without identifying its originator. In the same way, the literate people of the sixteenth century who came upon the proverb, in their turn, passed it on, with no attempt to identify either the immediate source of their knowledge of the saying or the original derivation. For them the saying was not a striking epigram of the Greeks or a piece of practical advice of the Romans, but was simply a wise and true observation on human life and, as such, the legitimate property of all men.

Two Renaissance Dialogues
in the Manner of Lucian

IF LUCIAN COULD HAVE been given the opportunity to choose the time and place in which he would spend his life, the odds are great that he would have chosen the age of the Renaissance in Italy, for he would have found the intellectual ferment and the sophisticated and cosmopolitan character of the humanists quite congenial. As it happened, however, Lucian was born in Samosata on the Euphrates about A.D. 115. Early in life he became a rhetorician and travelled through Greece, Italy, and even southern Gaul earning his living by his recitations. At the age of forty he settled in Athens where he studied philosophy and devoted himself to writing, chiefly on popular philosophical and literary themes. Witty and often irreverent, sceptical and cynical, with a contempt for sham and hypocrisy, he was the author of about a hundred compositions in Attic prose, ranging from his unorthodox *How to Write History*, an entertaining commentary on some of the contemporary historians, and *The Sale of Lives* (of the philosophers) in which the auctioneer finds it difficult to find buyers for even the best of the philosophers, to the *Voyage to the Lower World*, where the whole mythology surrounding death is ridiculed. Lucian's chief contribution is the satiric dialogue, best illustrated by his *Dialogues of the Dead* in which various historical and fictional characters reveal the pretences and vanities of living men, and the *Dialogues of the Gods* where the truth about some of the myths of the gods is exposed.

Lucian's remarkable fantasies, his clear and fast-moving style, his brilliant but biting wit, his bold unmasking of human self-deception, and his underlying purpose to make men realize their potential dignity were not fully appreciated until the time of the Renaissance. Then the Italian humanists recognized their spiritual kinship with this clever and brave critic of society. As soon as Lucian's works became available, they read them eagerly; the foremost scholars, including Filelfo, Poggio, Guarino, and Bruni, made Latin translations of some of them, and many more imitated his works.[1] Two of these men who were in part responsible for starting the great vogue for the works of Lucian were Giovanni Aurispa (1376?–1459) and Maffeo Vegio (1407–1458). Copies of their dialogues in the manner of Lucian are found in two fifteenth-century manuscripts in the Beinecke Library at Yale.

Aurispa,[2] a Sicilian humanist educated in Naples and later a teacher of Greek in Bologna and Florence, devoted his greatest efforts toward locating as many Greek literary manuscripts as possible. Two long sojourns—one of nine years and the other of three—spent in searching for manuscripts not only in Constantinople but all over the Byzantine Empire were very rewarding. In 1423 he returned to Venice with two hundred and thirty-eight Greek manuscripts, including the works of Aeschylus, Sophocles, Plato, Pindar, and Lucian.[3] Although he considered himself more of a book collector than a scholar, he did translate two of the dialogues of Lucian into Latin. One of these translations occurs in a Yale manuscript (Marston MS 63) written in Siena in 1465. It is a small volume of sixty-seven folios, written on paper in humanistic script, and bound in contemporary doeskin. The manuscript contains a representative selection of short works by early humanists. Aurispa's contribution (ff. 42^r–44^v) is a short dialogue called *Controversy between the Roman Scipio, Alexander of Macedon, and Hannibal of Carthage before Minos as to which of them deserves first place and is most worthy of praise*. The dialogue is modelled closely upon Lucian's *Dialogues of the Dead* XII (25). In both dialogues the debaters argue their own supremacy in the art of war and extol their own success. In the end, Lucian has Minos award the first place to the Greek Alexander, but for the Italian Aurispa, this seemed impossible, so he makes the judge award the prize to the Roman Scipio.[4] Also in the Beinecke Library there are two incunabular copies of Aurispa's second Lucianic dialogue: *How one can be carried across the Acheron alone and naked* (*Dialogus quomodo solus nudus per Acheronta transvehi potest*). It was edited by Paul Naivis and printed in Leipzig in 1490 and again in Deventer in 1497. Although the dialogue is credited to Lucian, Aurispa's Latin version is modelled only loosely upon Lucian's *Downward Journey*, in which the Cynic philosopher manages to talk Charon into taking him in his boat even though he does not have the necessary fare. The publication of this little book in the northern countries may have been one of the factors that stimulated unusual interest in Lucian among the German humanists. Eleven of these scholars made German translations of some of the dialogues. Among them, the *Dialogues of the Dead* by Johann Reuchlin (1495), the greatest Greek scholar of them all, was widely circulated. The *Epistolae obscurorum virorum* (1515), that vehement satire on some of the obscurantist theologians of Cologne, was written in part by Ulrich von Hutten who was influenced by some of Lucian's most cynical dialogues for his attacks.

Besides Aurispa, the other early Italian humanist who helped increase the popularity of Lucian's dialogues was Maffeo Vegio.[5] Born into a family of means, he was given every opportunity to acquire a good education. His early interest in literature led him to study at Milan, Pavia, Florence, and Rome. He came to count among his friends such outstanding scholars as Lorenzo Valla, Guarino of Verona, Aeneas Silvius Piccolomini, Flavio Biondo, Leonardo Bruni, and Ambrogio Traversari. Vegio had a remarkably wide acquaintance with Greek and Latin literature and an extensive knowledge of the writings of the Greek and the Latin Church Fathers. His own writings, begun in his school days, include early poetry in imitation of the ancient models, particularly Virgil, then essays, dialogues, epigrams, epistles, and, in middle life after his appointment as canon of the Basilica of St. Peter, hymns, psalms, liturgies, and lives of saints. The two of his works that have received the most attention in modern times are his *Libri XII Aeneidos Supplementum* and his *De educatione liberorum*. The first, written when Vegio was only twenty-one, is generally known as *The Thirteenth Book of the Aeneid*. It consists of six hundred and thirty lines of dactyllic hexameter, making what Vegio considered a more satisfactory ending to the epic. In it, Turnus, the last great enemy of the Trojans, is slain in battle and has an appropriate funeral; old Latinus of Laurentum gives his daughter Lavinia in marriage to Aeneas. After three happy years in a peaceful Italy, Aeneas dies and Jupiter receives his spirit into the realm of the stars. The other book, in prose, written in 1444, is a long treatise on the education of children, which stresses moral training along with physical and mental exercises. A timely and modified successor to the many treatises on the education of the prince written during the late Middle Ages, it was one of the first of the Renaissance discussion on the subject.

In 1452, Vegio wrote a very long dialogue, *Disputatio inter solem et terram et aruum* [Debate between the sun, the earth, and gold][6] on the question whether the upper part of the world represented by the sun, or the lower part represented by the earth and gold is of greater benefit to mankind. The Creator of the universe is judge and human beings constitute the jury. The dialogue does not follow any of Lucian's dialogues and is much more subtle than those written by Aurispa. It occurs in a Yale manuscript (Marston MS 91, ff. 131^r–166^v), a fine vellum and

℃ Maphei Vegij sua etate oratorū principis:inter inferiora cor=pora/scilicet Terram.Aurum/et supe riora/presertim Solem elegantissima simul et iocundissima disputatio.

Uenūdatur Parrhisijs Jn Sole Aureo vici sancti Jacobi Per ma gistrum Bertholdum Rembolt.

TITLE PAGE OF MAPHAEUS VEGIUS' *Disputatio.* (Paris, 1511)

Beinecke Rare Book and Manuscript Library, Yale University

paper volume that was copied in France in the fifteenth century.

In his dialogue, Vegio has Earth speak first. With great eloquence she tells of the beauty of her mountains and valleys, her woodlands and streams of the country with farms and orchards, and of the cities with their temples and palaces. Earth reminds the judges of her other great benefits to men in the abundance of fruits and grains and the variety of domestic animals. When Earth mentions the wonderful gift of the bees, she gives a long encomium on this marvellous little creature, following Virgil's fourth *Georgic*. After the speech is ended, it seems clear that Earth will be the winner, but the Sun is so confident of his superiority that he makes only a brief oration. He emphasizes the fact that men could enjoy none of the beauty or benefits of Earth without the light of the Sun. Then he continues as he calls attention to the wonderful arrangement of alternating day and night, and comments upon the remarkable arrangement of the seasons, all made possible by the Sun. What further could be said? If the dialogue had ended here, it would have been an unusually fine example of the medieval debate in the tradition of Alcuin's *Conflict between Spring and Winter* and Chaucer's *The Parliament of Fowls*. At this point, however, Gold insists loudly that he be given an opportunity to speak for himself. When the Judge agrees, Gold begins a brilliant oration which is twice as long as that of Earth. He first points out men's age-old veneration of gold since they made statues, shrines, and altars of the gods of that precious metal. Yet it is of far greater importance to men's lives, for without it there would not only be no commerce and industry, but none of the amenities of civilization would be possible. Even more significant, there would be no justice, no morality, no poetry, no philosophy. So convincing is Gold's subtle and specious reasoning, set forth with all the figures of rhetoric, that the admiring audience and even the Judge declare him the winner. Though Vegio never refers to Lucian, he has out-Lucianed the Greek satirist in his smooth presentation in painting black white. The early readers did not misunderstand his cleverness. In an edition of the dialogue printed in Paris in 1511,[7] the editor speaks of Vegio's masterful imitation of Lucian as he finds him noteworthy for his fluency, his versatility, and his artistry, and he characterizes him "the prince of orators" of his age. The printing of Vegio's dialogue in Paris and the earlier copying of the manuscript in France are indications of the reaction of the intellectuals in northwestern Europe to the dialogues of Lucian. Indeed, some of these scholars had already written original pieces in the manner of Lucian. Erasmus, for example, had published in 1509 his *Praise of Folly*, one of the greatest of the Lucianic satires.[8] This was followed by his *Colloquies*, dialogues full of wit and satiric barbs, and finally by his Latin translations of thirty of Lucian's works. Sir Thomas More contributed translations of three of the dialogues, and his own *Utopia* with its humor, irony, and cynicism was inspired by the dialogues of Lucian.

But Maffeo Vegio's Lucianic dialogue was best appreciated in Italy by his wide circle of friends among the humanists. As evidence of this one may cite a dialogue of Aeneas Silvius Piccolomini.[9] This dialogue is a discussion in defence of the *Donation of Constantine*, but it is introduced by a long preface full of reminiscences of Virgil, though in the spirit of Lucian. Presented in the form of a dream, in which incompatible features are accepted as normal, both the living and the dead are speakers, and the background is both pagan and Christian. St. Bernardino of Siena conducts Aeneas through the underworld where he meets Lorenzo Valla, Flavio Biondo, Petrus Noxetanus, secretary to Pope Nicholas V, Coluccio Salutati, Bruni, and Maffeo Vegio. As soon as they come to the underworld library, these men, all avid bibliophiles, fall into a lively discussion of countless ancient authors, from Homer to Quintilian. Vegio, however, is only concerned with finding the lost work of Cicero, *On the Republic*, which he thinks must surely be in the library. Even after he has been assured by Flavio Biondo that he has searched the library for this treasure, Vegio continues to lament the loss of this great book and somehow consoles himself by reciting a long passage on philosophy from Cicero's *Tusculan Disputations*.[10]

UNUSUAL ANIMALS IN BOOKS

THE OSTRICH. Sebastian Münster, *Cosmographia universalis* (Basel, 1550), p. 1150

Some Medieval Impressions
of the Ostrich

My child, the Duck-billed Platypus
A sad example sets for us:
From him we learn how Indecision
Of character provokes Derision.
This vacillating Thing, you see,
Could not decide which he would be,
Fish, Flesh or Fowl, and chose all three.[1]

A MATTER WHICH THE MODERN VERSIFIER treats with wit and
levity, the anatomy, physical appearance, mental capacity, and
behavior of animals and birds, was considered by medieval men
as the proper province of the moralists who could draw from this
rich field important lessons for human beings. Many of the tales
they told derive ultimately, of course, from the Aesopian corpus,
perhaps by way of the Latin version of Phaedrus or the later
reworkings of Babrius, Avianus, and the so-called Pseudo-
Romulus. Frequently the medieval writers present this material
not as fables, but as natural history, in bestiaries which were

chiefly the outgrowth of the Latin translation of the fourth-century Greek work known as *Physiologus*. In general, the commonplace birds and animals appear as they do in the old stories, but the unusual creatures challenged the imagination of the writers, and one finds some original descriptions and some singular lessons to be learned from them. Among the unfamiliar creatures, few stimulated their curiosity more than the ostrich.

Tacitus' dictum, "The unknown always passes for the marvellous" (*Agricola*, 30), seems particularly applicable to the ostrich as treated by the men of the Middle Ages. Since very few people in Europe had seen an ostrich, writers were obliged to depend upon the descriptions given in Pliny, Isidore of Seville, and *Physiologus*, their most easily accessible sources. What chiefly caught their fancy and even offended them was the apparently dual nature of the creature, for it has the characteristics of both bird and animal.

The writers of the early bestiaries were given a clear mandate for using the animals for the purpose of moralizing, as one sees in Job when he says, "Ask the beasts and they shall teach thee, and the fowls of the air and they shall tell thee" (12 : 7), an injunction literally interpreted by three writers who seem to express the thinking of their contemporaries. The first of the three treatments of the subject is a bestiary, originating in the eleventh century but preserved in a twelfth-century manuscript from the abbey of Revesby in Lincolnshire and now in the University Library, Cambridge.[2] The second is a work entitled *Moralitates de avibus*, by Cardinal Hugo de Folieto, whose life covered the first three-quarters of the twelfth century. It is preserved in a number of manuscripts, one of which, copied in the twelfth century, is now in the Beinecke Library at Yale.[3] The text is given in the *Patrologia Latina* (177, 14–164), with the writings of Hugo of St. Victor. The third is a collection of one hundred and twenty-two fables, entiled *Dialogus creaturarum*, which is often attributed to an unidentified Nicolaus Pergamenus, a scholar possibly from Macedonia, living in the fourteenth century. The work is preserved in several manuscripts in the Bibliothèque Nationale,[4] and there are a number of vernacular translations that were published in the fifteenth century, of which the best-known is an early English translation which was reprinted by J. Hastlewood in 1816. The Latin text is available in a modern German edition.[5]

These writers assume several "facts" commonly accepted about the nature of the ostrich: the creature is very large, with wings and feathers, but it cannot fly; it has powerful cloven hoofs like the camel and can outrun a horse; the female lays eggs in the sand, covers them, and then abandons them. These abnormal features provide material for moralizing. To explain the paradox of a great bird equipped with wings and feathers, but without the ability to fly, Nicolaus has a dialogue entitled, "Concerning the ostrich and the surgeon."[6] In it he says that once there was a fine and beautiful ostrich that had very strong and handsome wings, but there were two feathers turned backward, a circumstance that hurt his vanity and grieved him very much. So he went to a surgeon and asked him to amputate the two feathers. After the surgeon carried out the operation, he applied such a strong ointment that all the other wing feathers fell out and the bird could never fly again. The poor creature mourned the rest of its life and warned others against the same kind of fate, saying, "Let us remain as God has created us; let us never change ourselves." Nicolaus enlarges upon the lesson to be learned from this experience: if some people are so vain and conceited that they are troubled by a minor physical blemish, far from giving thanks to their Creator, they try in every possible way to have the defect remedied; but if they have some defects of the soul, they make no attempt to have them remedied.

Hugo de Folieto sees in the physical characteristics of the ostrich another salutary lesson for men.[7] The great bird has strong wings covered with beautiful feathers but it cannot achieve what these advantages should provide, namely flight, hence it is not what it appears to be. In this way it is like many men who appear to be Christians, who speak of holiness, but there is no holiness in their actions. They are hypocrites. Peter

Riga, also, in his versified explanation of the Bible,[8] condemns
the ostrich as a hypocrite because it pretends to be flying when
it is simply running swiftly, assisted by the motion of its wings.
In his *Speculum sapientiae*, Bishop Cyrillus uses the ostrich in two
fables as a notorious example to warn people against pre-
sumptuousness and against the desire to seem what one is not.[9]

A third stricture often made on the ostrich is that of stupidity.
Job had remarked on the strange habit of the bird of abandoning
its eggs, but he explains, "God hath deprived her of wisdom,
neither hath he imparted to her understanding" (39:17). The
author of the English bestiary, however, shows more knowledge
of the actual situation. He says that the bird watches the sky and
waits until the Pleiades appear before it lays eggs. Then it covers
them with sand, but with the clemency of the weather in June,
the sun and the warm sand incubate the eggs. Herein lies a
salutary lesson for men. "Now if the ostrich knows its time and
seasons, and, disregarding earthly things, cleaves to the heavenly
ones—even unto the forgetting of its own offspring—how
much the more should you, O Man, strive after the reward of the
starry calling, on account of which God was made man that he
might enlighten you from the powers of darkness and place you
with the chiefs of his people in the glorious kingdom of
heaven."[10]

The two twelfth-century manuscripts in which the earlier
works have been preserved contain illustrations. The artist who
pictured the ostrich in Hugo de Folieto's work on birds (f. 7ʳ)
had no access to any realistic picture or any fuller description, yet
somehow he was able to catch the essential features of the bird.
The artist who illustrated the Cambridge bestiary drew a charming scene, framed in a circle, of two large birds with short necks
and short legs, one standing behind the other. The bird in back
is looking upward beyond the oval frame toward a very large
star with a flaming aureole, while the other is covering three
great eggs with sand, again outside of the circular frame.[11] The
third illustration is found in a nineteenth-century reprinting of
an undated early English translation, entitled *Dialogues of*

Creatures Moralyzed.[12] Here the ostrich is a large bird, as tall as a man, but with short legs and very distinctly cloven hoofs and a short neck. It is confronting the surgeon who has a jar of ointment in his hand. The ostrich holds a large horseshoe in its beak.

The appearance of the horseshoe with the ostrich is an indication of a change in emphasis after the twelfth century, from the vanity, pride, hypocrisy, and stupidity of the creature to certain physiological traits. Europe had had an opportunity to read of far places and exotic animals in such works as those of Marco Polo. Also available were the encyclopedias of scholars like Vincent of Beauvais, as well as the work of Albertus Magnus, *On Animals.* One of the "facts" about the ostrich which Albertus Magnus had tried vainly to refute (XXIII.139) by describing his experiments with the creatures, but which Vincent emphatically affirmed, was that the great bird ate and digested iron.[13] This idea made a strong impression upon the later medieval writers. Since, for most people, iron would be known in the form of some familiar and useful object forged from the ore, it is not surprising that they often pictured the ostrich holding a horseshoe. Other iron objects also represented in the same way include nails and chains. For example, on the heraldic badge of Anne of Bohemia, wife of Richard II, there is depicted a tall ostrich with a crown and a fetterlock around its neck and a large nail in its beak.[14] This practice continued into the Renaissance, as one sees in a magnificent woodcut of the great bird in Sebastian Münster's *Cosmographia universalis.* In discussing Africa, the famous German humanist mentions the ostrich's habit of eating iron. He illustrates the text with the representation of a very large bird with an unusually long neck, tall legs and strong feet, beautiful plumes, and a large beak in which it holds a great key, while at its feet lies a large horseshoe.[15]

The tradition of the iron-eating ostrich persisted into the sixteenth century, as one sees in Shakespeare's *II Henry VI* (4.10) where Jack Cade says, "I'll make thee eat iron like an ostrich, and swallow my sword like a great pin, ere thou and I part."

Coincidentally, there is a fine carved representation of an ostrich carrying a horseshoe in its mouth on a misericord in a choir stall in the Church of the Holy Trinity in Stratford-on-Avon.[16] A number of comprehensive books on natural history produced during the next two centuries repeat the old story that ostriches eat and digest iron, in spite of Sir Thomas Browne's publication of his experiments which demonstrated that the bird cannot digest iron.[17] During this same period the possibilities of the ostrich in symbolic representation were widely explored. So the contemporary emblem books show a variety of ways in which the bird serves to illustrate some noble motto, but most of them are concerned with its iron-eating habit. In one, for example, the motto "Sic nutriuntur fortes" is illustrated by a representation of an ostrich with a horseshoe in its beak.[18] Another motto in the same collection reads "Spiritus durissima coquit." Two more variations on the same theme bear the legends "Dura vinco" and "Nil durum indigestum."[19] In every instance they strees the qualities of courage, endurance, and spiritual strength, and all credit the bird as setting an example beneficial to human beings.

At the present time, however, divested of all the magic and mystery long associated with it, and even bereft of its usefulness as an object lesson, much less as an example, the ostrich has been reduced to an ignominious role. Two aspects of its behavior are stressed to make it the perfect exemplar of stupidity. On the supposition that when outflanked by an enemy it hides its head in a bush (a most effective camouflage) because it thinks that if it cannot see, it cannot be seen, the man who refuses to face a difficult situation is called an ostrich. Again, because the ostrich eats gravel and even bits of metal (to aid in its peculiar process of digestion), the glutton who eats rough and harsh food is said to have the stomach of an ostrich. So it is that the ostrich has lost all of the romance that in the Middle Ages surrounded this mysterious creature, half bird, half camel, the struthiocamelus.

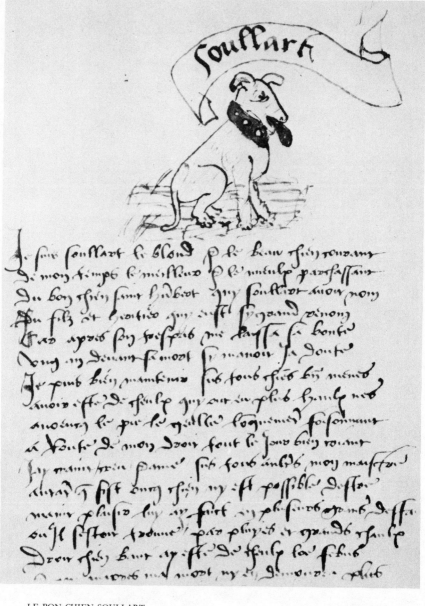

LE BON CHIEN SOULLART

Beinecke Rare Book and Manuscript Library, Yale University, MS 121, f. 59^r

Le Bon Chien Soullart

ONE OF THE MOST MEMORABLE EPISODES in the *Odyssey* is the account of the recognition of the hero upon his return home by his faithful dog, Argos, or Swift-foot. Odysseus, successful in disguising his identity from his loyal old servant, Eumaeus, is deeply moved at the feeble welcome given him by the noble animal, which he himself had bred and which for twenty years had proved himself the fleetest and keenest of hounds, now lying neglected in the dung of the farmyard. While Odysseus manages to conceal his tears, the aged Argos falls dead from the unusual strain upon his old heart.

Of all the handsome, swift, and loyal dogs that have followed Argos during the course of history, few are more deserving of remembrance than Soullart, a noble hound in the court of Louis XI of France. Lacking a Homer, Soullart himself wrote a poem in which he records his ancestry, his appearance, his prowess in the hunt, and the progeny he left to win acclaim for their exploits in hunting.

The Beinecke Library possesses one of the best of the four

manuscripts in which Soullart's poem is preserved. This (MS 121) is a small volume of sixty leaves, written in French toward the end of the fifteenth century. The main text in the manuscript is the anonymous work entitled *Le livre du roy Modus* [commonly translated The Book of King Method], the oldest book on hunting in French, which presents a philosophical and moralizing as well as practical treatment of the subject. The next to the last leaf of the manuscript contains Soullart's poem of sixty verses of twelve syllables in rhyming couplets, headed by a drawing of a dog bearing the caption "Soullart." The poem is followed by a list of thirty-two names of dogs, each with the female version. In the list the name "Soullart" appears as number twenty-three.

The text of the Yale manuscript is complete and generally good, though a number of readings differ from those of the other fifteenth-century manuscript (Paris, B.N. 12398). More pronounced differences occur in a seventeenth-century version (The Hague, 78 e 37), which has several lacunae and a number of poor readings. A fourth manuscript (Turin, Archivio di Stato, VII.31) is very late and incomplete. An incunable edition was printed in Paris about 1494, but unfortunately it provides a very poor text. The title of the poem varies: in the manuscript in The Hague it is "Epitaphe de Souillart," which is obviously incorrect, since the dog speaks of himself as enjoying life; in the Paris manuscript the title is "Soullart le blanc," and appears above a fine sketch of a spirited dog held by a leash, all of which is enclosed in a decorative border. The incunabular version bears the title: *Les ditz du bon chien Souillart: qui fut au roi Loys de France.*

The poem has been published twice since the fifteenth century, first by Baron Jérome Picheron in his edition of *La Chasse du grand Seneschal de Normandye* (Paris, 1858), using only the incunable as the basis for his text. In 1959, Gunnar Tilander published a critical edition from the four manuscripts and the incunable. Here, then, one can be confident that the text accurately represents the sayings of the good dog Soullart.[1]

Soullart begins his poem by giving his name and stating simply that he is handsome and white and that he enjoys the reputation of being the best hunting dog of his time. His sire, also named Soullart, was of the breed known as St. Hubert, from the abbey in the Ardennes dedicated to the patron of hunting.[2] Himself renowned for his prowess in the field, he had the satisfaction of training his very promising offspring. The younger Soullart asserts his supremacy in every respect over all the other aristocratic hunting dogs of his day. His love and respect for his master are unparalleled, as he has demonstrated by the pleasure he has afforded him as well as by his resourcefulness in rescuing him from dangerous situations on the hunt. He claims to be one of the excellent dogs praised by Gaston Phoebus in his book on hunting and dogs.[3] He foresees that after his death there will be no dog of such great competence, except his own progeny, of which there are twenty-two, seven of which he names. He himself has never been surpassed for his speed, his hardiness, and his expertness in hunting deer. He has outraced the swiftest horses, even when his master spurred them so hard that they fell dead under him. He has known three masters: Louis of France, Gaston the seneschal, and the grand seneschal, Jacques. Now that he is old, his master permits him to take his ease, with plenty of good food and a fine warm bed of clean straw in his own bedroom. Soullart proudly wears a collar decorated with the crosses of the arms of the Brézé family. Finally, he prays for the repose of the soul of King Louis and of the seneschal, Gaston. He says that he expects to end his days in the care of his present master.

Soullart nowhere reveals who actually penned his poem for him, but perhaps he expected his readers to assume that it was his beloved and devoted master, Jacques de Brézé, "le grand seneschal de Normandie," noted for his interest in hunting and for his poetry. It is the only assumption one can make now, for Jacques de Brézé as owner not only knew more about him than anyone else, but would have been the one person chiefly interested in composing some suitable memorial for such a superior stag hound. In two of the manuscripts and in the incunable, Soullart's poem occurs after Jacques de Brézé's long poem, "La Chasse," and the two poems show similar metrical and linguistic traits. The date of the composition of Soullart's poem, if it was written by Brézé, can be fixed between the years 1483, the death of Louis XI, and 1490, which marked Brézé's own death.

An evaluation of Soullart's place among hunting dogs is made by Jacaues du Fouilloux in his popular book, *La Vénerie*, written about the middle of the sixteenth century. Chapter II of the book is devoted to the history of the white hunting dogs, originally stag hounds.[4] Du Fouilloux says that Soullart (whom he calls Souillard), first of his breed, came into prominence when a poor gentleman offered him to Louis XI of France. The King, however, had no interest in any but gray dogs, of which he had a large pack. His seneschal, Gaston, who happened to be present and knew the King's preference, begged that he be given the dog in order that he might present the beautiful white animal to the wisest lady in the kingdom. When Louis asked who that lady might be, Gaston replied that she was the King's own daughter, Anne de Bourbon. While the King was bound to agree, he said that a more accurate statement would be that she was less foolish than others, for actually there was no wise woman in the world. In the end Anne did not receive the dog, for Jacques de Brézé, the grand seneschal of Normandy, importuned the owner so insistently that Gaston felt obliged to accede to his wish.

By way of parenthesis, one may note that the dog would have been a most appropriate gift for Anne, and, besides, Jacques was well aware of her interest in dogs and her skill in hunting. He himself had noted these traits in his long poem, "La Chasse,"[5] which describes a stag hunt in which Anne took part. He speaks with great admiration of her beauty and physical perfection, her endowment with all good gifts so that she was a masterpiece of God's creation. In addition to all this, she was superb in the sport of hunting. Later, after Anne became regent of France during the minority of her brother, Charles VIII (1483–1491), Jacques wrote in her honor a poem entitled "Louanges de Madame Anne de France, Duchesse de Bourbon."[6] In it Jacques shows that he agrees with the seneschal, Gaston, that Anne is the wisest of women, for he emphasizes her wisdom and her other excellences: besides being remarkable for her beauty, her goodness, her charity and gentleness, and her strength of character, she is a veritable Minerva, and indeed, the wisest sibyl of her time.

In his account of Soullart's life, Du Fouilloux reports that the dog was prized by his new master, Jacques. In the Brézé kennels Soullart sired a number of superior hunting hounds. Eventually, Anne de Bourbon heard of the excellence of this new breed of hunting dog and procured a number of the puppies. Thereafter every effort was made to improve the breed in appearance, strength, endurance, and effectiveness in hunting, so that in a surprisingly short time these white hounds became the favorites of princes. Under Francis I, one of these white dogs was designated "un vrai chien du Roy." [7] The large, powerfully built dog pictured at the head of the chapter in the 1562 edition of Du Fouilloux's book differs greatly from his ancestor, Soullart, the small white dog wearing the collar with the crosses of the Brézé crest, drawn above his poem in the Yale manuscript.

The Yale manuscript in itself is not without interest. It is written on paper in dark ink, in a cursive script. Two watermarks in the paper show that it was produced in northern France toward the end of the fifteenth century. Fifty-eight leaves, rubricated and decorated with penwork initials, contain the treatise Le livre du roy Modus, into which is incorporated a long poem on the relative merits of hunting with dogs and with hawks. Leaf fifty-nine, in the same hand, contains the Soullart poem followed by a list of names of dogs. The last leaf is blank except for a small drawing of a lion. Although the manuscript was copied in France, the first indication of ownership shows that it was early in England, for the signature, "Laurens Nowell 1564," appears on the first and on the penultimate leaves. (Laurence Nowell, dean of Winchester, was noted as an antiquarian with a great interest in manuscripts.) In modern times the manuscript was rebound in brown half-leather. The volume was still in England in the twentieth century, as a note in pencil on the flyleaf is signed, "W.G. Lambarde April, 1913," and the Lambarde bookplate appears on the inside front cover. The next indication of ownership is the bookplate of C.F.G.R. Schwerdt, and the manuscript is described in the catalogue of Schwerdt's great collection of sporting books.[8] When that collection was dispersed, the manuscript was sold by E.P. Goldschmidt to David Wagstaff for his excellent collection of sporting books. It came to Yale in 1946 as the gift of Mrs. Wagstaff.

The dog whose poem has been under consideration shared a trait of character with all good dogs, namely, loyalty to his master. In Homer's Argos this is demonstrated in his happy recognition of Odysseus, the strain of which cost him his life. In Soullart, the expression of loyalty is more subtle, for the faithful hound speaks only in praise of his master, Jacques de Brézé, and nowhere even hints that it was because of Brézé that he was prevented from going to the royal kennels as the special hunting dog of Anne de Bourbon.

The American Unicorn

IN EUROPE, THE UNICORN had been known for over twenty centuries before it was first reported in the forests of North America. The traditional animal had been described by such scientific writers as Aristotle (*Historia animalium*, II.2.8 and VI.36), and Albertus Magnus (*De animalibus historia*, XX, tract. 2, cap. 1); it had been mentioned by travelers like Ctesias, a Greek physician in the court of the Persian ruler Darius, who cites an eyewitness account of the animal in India (*Indica*, fr. 25 and 33), and Bernard of Breydenbach, who, on a pilgrimage from Mainz to the Holy Land, caught sight of a unicorn on a mountain peak in the Sinai.[1] Information about the animal had been made generally available by compilers like the Swiss encyclopedist Conrad Gesner,[2] and the English scholar Edward Topsell,[3] who, in their great collections, presented the findings of earlier explorers and scientists on this subject. Of course, from early medieval times the unicorn had been better known as a creature of fantasy and romance, of allegory and symbolism, depicted in carvings on wood and stone, on tapestries, and on coats of arms. Our concern here, however, is with the actual animal in its native habitat.

The first intimation that the unicorn existed in America came from sixteenth-century explorers. Richard Hakluyt, in his account of the English navigators, records two pieces of evidence. From the account by Sir John Hawkins of his voyages to the New World in 1564, Hakluyt quotes a passage relating to Florida in which the inhabitants are described as wearing pieces of unicorn horn in their necklaces.

> Of these unicornes they have many; for that they doe affirm it to be a beast with one horne, which coming to the river to drinke, putteth the same into the water before he drinketh. Of this unicornes horne there are of our company, that having gotten the same of the Frenchmen, brought home thereof to show.[4]

Another English explorer, John Davis, in his efforts to find a northwest passage to India, visited the east coast of North America. In the account of his experiences preserved by Hakluyt, under date of 14 June 1584, Davis describes gifts offered by the natives, among them "... a darte with a bone in it, of a piece of Unicornes horne; as I did judge."[5] This slight testimony and that of Sir John Hawkins would seem to indicate that both travelers brought their belief in unicorns with them from Europe.

It remained for a Dutch geographer to discover and describe the native American unicorn. The great work of Arnoldus Montanus (1625–83) was published in three different versions between 1671 and 1673. The original edition, in Dutch, was printed in Amsterdam by Jacob van Meurs. Entitled *De Nieuwe en onbekende Weereld: of Beschryving van America en 't Zuid-land*, it is a large folio volume containing information about North, South, and Central America and the adjacent islands. It includes descriptions of the physical features of the various countries, the native inhabitants and their customs, the animals and vegetation, along with accounts of the early explorations of the territories,

E AMERICAN UNICORN. Arnoldus Montanus, *De Nieuwe en onbekende Weereld*
msterdam, 1671), p. 126   Beinecke Rare Book and Manuscript Library, Yale University

the colonists, and the settlements that had been established. The book is illustrated with seven portraits, including those of Columbus and Magellan, thirty-two large engravings of the most important sites and settlements, and sixteen maps, of which the most remarkable is a very large one of the western hemisphere. The work is dedicated to Ioan Maurits, prince of Nassau, whose portrait appears in the book. In treating North America, the author devotes a large section (pp. 123–134) to New Netherland.

The second version is an English translation, unusual in that it appeared in the same year (1671) as the original text. John Ogilby, the enterprising printer who had already published large volumes on China and Japan translated from Montanus' *Atlas Chinensis* and *Atlas Japannensis* and from Olfert Dapper's *Africa* and *Asia*, seems to have made his English translation from Montanus' manuscript. His book uses the same illustrations and maps as the first edition, printed from the original plates (owned by Jacob van Meurs). Issued in London, it is called *America: Being the Latest and Most Accurate Description of the New World*. In content it follows Montanus' text except that descriptions of several English colonies are taken from English sources. Of course the section on New Netherland (pp. 168–182) is translated from Montanus and is illustrated by the same two engravings as in the Dutch first edition.

The third version of Montanus was printed by van Meurs in Amsterdam in 1673. It is a faithful German translation, with the title: *Die unbekannte Neue Welt, oder Beschreibung des Welt-teils Amerika*. Except for the omission of the dedication to and portrait of the prince of Nassau, the book follows the original exactly and contains all the illustrations and maps. At the end of the long descriptive title, the words "durch Dr. O. D." were added by the translator to signify that this book was included in the great collection of geographical works made by Dr. Olfert Dapper.[6] With this sponsorship, the German version became the most widely circulated of the three texts. Since it is an exact translation of the Dutch, the passage on New Netherland is the same as in the original.

In the Dutch edition the section devoted to the settlement is preceded by an engraving of New Amsterdam with its houses, docks, church, and warehouses on the banks of the river, where several ships ride at anchor. The author gives the boundaries of the colony as Virginia on the southwest and New England on the northeast, the river Canada on the north, and the Ocean on the southeast. He then describes the physical features of the colony, the rivers and harbor, the trees and wild vegetation, as well as the cultivated plants and vegetables. He discusses the native Indians and the animals and birds found in New Netherland, devoting one section of his exposition (pp. 125–127) to "Strange beasts," and here mentioning in some detail the elk, the deer, the civet cat, the beaver, and the unicorn. The rest of the chapter is concerned with the history of the settlement and the manner of life of the settlers.

Since our interest is in the unicorn, I give an English translation by an anonymous nineteenth-century scholar of Montanus' account:

> On the borders of *Canada* animals are now and again seen, somewhat resembling a horse; they have cloven hoofs, shaggy manes, a horn right out of the forehead, a tail like that of a wild pig, black eyes, a stag's neck & love the gloomiest wildernesses; are shy of each other so that the male never feeds with the female except when they associate for the purposes of increase. Then they lay aside their ferocity; as soon as the rutting season is past, they again not only become wild but even attack their own.[7]

It would be natural to assume that the description came from the inaccurate reporting of some fleeting impression of a solitary deer-like creature in a dense forest, if it were not followed by a long discussion of the civet cat, which is certainly the African animal confused with the American muskrat. Here[8] the author quotes Pliny, Cardanus, and Julius Scaliger Matthiolus as authorities on the subject of the civet, derived from these animals in Africa and Asia. Thus also, although the author does not acknowledge it, the source of his information on the habits of the unicorn is the *Historia animalium* (VI.20) of Aelian, a second-century rhetorician who made a collection of facts and anecdotes about animals. Aelian was describing the unicorn of India, which may have been the rhinoceros.

Accompanying Montanus' text and illustrating the passage on the strange animals of America, there is a large engraving (p. 126) in which the unicorn holds a central position.[9] A very large eagle with outspread wings stands on his back as he, a powerful, horse-like creature, charges a great elk with long branching antlers, who, in turn, attacks a smaller animal, which may be a deer. In the foreground are a beaver and civet cat, confronting each other with hostility. These are all set against a background of hills and of trees, including four which resemble date palms.

Although described and pictured in *De Nieuwe en onbekende Weereld* as living in the wild country of the northern border of New Netherland, this American unicorn apparently made little impression upon the settlers of the New World. Ironically, it was the European unicorn that played a role in the official life of the colony. In 1687, not long after the publication of Montanus' book, in the reign of James II, a great seal for the "Province of New York in America" was adopted for use on all state documents. Since the design for the seal became standardized in the reign of William and Mary, and was used until 1767 in the reign of George III, it is the one that is best known. The obverses of the six great seals differ, of course, with the reigning monarchs, but all represent the king or queen accepting gifts, often wampum and a beaver skin, from two kneeling Indians. The reverses remain essentially constant. Near the edge an inscription reads: "Sigillum Provinc. Nostr. Nov. Ebor. [etc.] in America." In the center, the shield with the royal arms is enclosed by the royal garter with the name of the monarch. Above the shield is the royal crown and beneath is the motto. The shield is upheld by two supporters, the crowned lion, and the unicorn with an elaborate collar and long chain.[10] So it happened that, as the American unicorn disappeared into the northern forests, the English unicorn was being stamped upon all state documents that affected the lives of the colonists of New York.

RARE BOOKS FROM THE STILES LIBRARY

Abiel Holmes'
Life of Ezra Stiles

ANYONE WHO HAS HAD the persistence to read through the modern three-volume edition of *The Literary Diary of Ezra Stiles*[1] will agree that in that vast storehouse of information there is material for many biographies of the famous diarist. These might include: *Ezra Stiles, Theologian and Pastor*; *Ezra Stiles, Amateur Scientist*; *Ezra Stiles, President of Yale College*, and *Ezra Stiles and the Intellectual and Political Leaders of his Day*. The first biography in this series was written in 1798 by the person best qualified to do it, Stiles' son-in-law, the Reverend Abiel Holmes, who gave it the general title *The Life of Ezra Stiles, D.D., LL.D.*,[2] though it might well have been called *The Spiritual Pilgrimage of Ezra Stiles*. Recently this biography and the other suggested ones were most skillfully incorporated into a comprehensive critical study of Ezra Stiles entitled *The Gentle Puritan* by Edmund S. Morgan of Yale.[3] Though Holmes' work has thus been superseded, because it is an authentic "period piece" presenting Stiles as his age would have him remembered, it has seemed worthwhile to consider its contents in some detail.[4]

Abiel Holmes (1763–1837) was a friend of Stiles all of his adult life. Born in Woodstock, Connecticut, the son of David Holmes who had served as a surgeon in the Revolutionary War, he entered Yale at the age of fifteen and was graduated in the class of 1783. His career at Yale can be traced by a number of entries in Stiles' *Diary* in which Holmes appears in class lists, in several notices for special examinations, then among those taking final examinations, and on whom degrees were conferred.[5] Holmes, in the preface of his *Life* (iii), states that he had been a pupil of Stiles, certainly in Ecclesiastical History and probably in Hebrew. What impressed Stiles most was that Holmes, in his sophomore year, was admitted into Communion, along with another undergraduate, Stiles himself administering the Sacrament.[6]

Two years after his graduation, Holmes was called to become pastor of a Congregational church in Midway, Georgia. He applied to the Council of Ministers of New Haven and, upon due consideration by some of the most esteemed ministers of the state, his petition was granted and he underwent a careful examination of his theological position. In his *Diary* Stiles gives a full account of the ordination that occurred in New Haven the day after Commencement, that is, September 17, 1785.[7] He himself ordained Holmes, offered the ordination prayer, and laid the solemn charge of ministry upon him. After a year in Georgia, Holmes accepted an invitation to spend the year as tutor at Yale, and then he resumed his pastoral duties in the South. In the summer of 1790 he was back in Connecticut visiting his old home in Woodstock and friends in New Haven where he was invited to preach in the Yale Chapel. On August 29, Stiles' daughter Mary, generally known as Polly, was married to Holmes.[8] In September the young couple sailed for Georgia, but the climate proved harmful to Holmes' health, so they returned to New England, and Holmes, shortly after, was established in the First Church in Cambridge, where he served

for thirty-seven years. In 1795, both Holmes' wife and her
father, Ezra Stiles, died. Friends persuaded Holmes to write the
life of Ezra Stiles. Shortly thereafter he started work on a
comprehensive study of the early history of the American
continent. In 1805 he published a two-volume work, *American
Annals or a Chronological History of America from its Discovery in
MCCCCXCII to MDCCCVI*, and in 1820 a new edition called
*The Annals of America, from the Discovery by Columbus in the Year
1492 to the Year 1820*. As a member of the Massachusetts
Historical Society, he published a great many articles of antiquarian interest. Holmes married Sarah Wendell in 1801 and one
of their five children was Oliver Wendell Holmes.

Holmes had the highest possible qualifications for writing an
understanding and sympathetic account of the life of Ezra Stiles.
These would include his long friendship with Dr. Stiles, his
relationship by marriage, their common intellectual and social
background, and his experience as a student at Yale, in addition
to his having the same profession. Yet Holmes was in possession
of an even more remarkable and valuable asset for the task.
When Stiles died, he stipulated in his will that his cabinet of
manuscripts, consisting of forty volumes, should be given into
the keeping of the Reverend Abiel Holmes for ten years, after
which they were to be deposited with the archives of Yale
College in the President's house. The manuscripts consisted of
fourteen volumes of his *Literary Diary* from 1769 to 1793, four
volumes of his *Itineraries*, five volumes of his *Thermo Register*, a
daily recording of temperatures and meteorological phenomena
from 1762 to 1793, one volume on *The Culture of Silk*, one with a
list of New England churches and ministers, and several volumes
of sermons, letters, and other miscellaneous material which Stiles
had collected during his lifetime. With all of this material
Holmes undertook writing the biography of Stiles.

With excellent judgment, Holmes chose to focus attention
upon the two most important aspects of Stiles' life—his
unceasing efforts to understand Christian theology in order to
develop and purify his own spiritual state, and his endless labors

on behalf of his parishioners. These concerns were also most closely related to Holmes' own experiences, and they were the ones that his generation would most appreciate. He justifies his emphasis on religion in his biography of a man of letters and science as well as of religion. "Religion was indelibly wrought, like Phidias' name in his shield, into the character which it delineates; and that, in the judgment of the compiler, the union of Piety with Learning forms the sublimest human character (vi)."

In his preface (iv) he says that it was his aim "to make the President, as far as possible, his own biographer" by quoting extensively from Stiles' writings. Of Stiles' early life, Holmes is satisfied with recording the facts that he was born in North Haven on December 10, 1727, the son of a minister, brought up in a home where books were readily available, that he became interested in learning and was ready for college at the age of twelve. He entered Yale at fifteen, and there devoted his attention to science and mathematics as well as church history, and was graduated as one of the leading students. Soon after, he was received into the church by his father. He was fortunate enough to have a year of postgraduate study at the college. Little is recorded of his academic work, but his rules of conduct which he drew up for himself indicate that his moral and spiritual development were of great concern to him (16–17). In 1749, he was chosen a tutor at Yale. At the same time, Dr. Franklin sent an electrical apparatus to Yale which enabled Stiles to perform "the first electrical experiments made in New-England" (19). The year was also memorable because he received a degree of master of arts and was granted a licence to preach by the New Haven Association of Ministers. When he found that the life of a preacher was too taxing to his health, he decided upon a career in law. After studying at Yale, he took the lawyer's oath in 1753 and practiced for two years. An improvement in his health influenced him to return to his first choice of the ministry, and he accepted a call to the Second

Congregational Church in Newport, Rhode Island. He was ordained in 1755.

For Holmes' purpose, a long Birth-Day Memoir, written by Stiles in 1767, is quoted in its entirety (32–43) because it contains Stiles' own analysis of his spiritual progress from childhood acceptance of the tenets of the Christian religion, through the dark days of doubt and scepticism during his post-college years, to his final triumphant affirmation of faith. The biographer has thereafter included Stiles' Birth-Day Reflections for almost every year, beginning in 1772, thus providing clear testimony to the continued spiritual growth and refinement of a dedicated and grateful Christian. One of the last Reflections was written in 1793 when Stiles was sixty-six years old and aware that his life was nearly over. His concluding sentences indicate his calm acceptance, as he says, "I have blessings in my family, and abundant reason for gratitude to the Most High, for continuing a life so useful. I desire renewedly to devote myself to God, and commit myself to his care, protection, and blessing. May I be prepared for eternity" (324–325).

Holmes emphasizes the fact that for Stiles there was a lifelong search to support and strengthen his religious beliefs. The biographer quotes a long passage in which Stiles records the various standard works of Protestant theology which he studied during several distressing years of scepticism (43–54). The passage is followed by a quotation from a discourse that Stiles prepared after his ordination in which he joyously affirms his complete acceptance of Christian revelation (59–63). Stiles' continued search for light on the background of Christianity led him to learn Hebrew, Arabic, Syriac, and Armenian and to read texts relating to Old Testament history (128–131). In order to understand the Bible more completely, Stiles turned his attention to the archaeology of the Holy Land. He wrote extensively to missionaries and travellers in the East in an effort to discover the answer to such questions as the fate of the Ten Tribes of Israel (158–162, 331–332). His inquiries went to such

diverse lands as the countries bordering on the Caspian Sea and
Abyssinia as he continued this investigation throughout his life,
enlarging the area of his search until, at the age of sixty-seven, he
was able to say that he had explored America, Europe, Asia,
Africa, China, India, and Tibet (320–326).

Although Stiles remained firmly committed to Con-
gregationalism, he consistently studied the various other forms
and tenets of Christian belief. Theology was his favorite subject
(355). He made a great effort to collect all of the patristic texts he
could locate; he studied not only the Latin Fathers, but the
Greek as well. He mentions Basil, Gregory of Nazianzum,
Chrysostom, and Cyprian (105), and again Eusebius, Justin
Martyr, and Origen (104), as authors whose works he found of
interest and importance. One of the Greek writers on theology
whom Stiles particularly admired was Dionysius the Areopagite
whom he mentions with great respect in his *Diary*.[9] Holmes
reports that in 1793 Stiles translated two letters of Dionysius on
the miraculous eclipse at the time of the Saviour's Crucifixion.
Holmes found this translation, and a dissertation to prove the
authenticity of the letters, in the cabinet of manuscripts that
Stiles had left to him with instructions to correct and publish
them (323–324).

Holmes admires not only Stiles' catholicity in his intellectual
search into the history of Christian thought, but also his in-
vestigations into the other great religions of his time. He looked
into the beliefs of the Mohammedans and the Hindus; he was
particularly eager to study the Vedas and other religious writings
in Sanskrit (134–136) to try to discover some link between them
and ancient Hebrew literature. Holmes paraphrases a Latin letter
of Stiles to M. de Sevigny, a chaplain in the French army, in
which he says, "That he has acquired much knowledge from
great and learned men, of all sects of Christianity, nay from
Deists, from Mohometans, and even from the disciples of Bonzes
and Brahmans. That the time has, or ought to have, arrived,
when religious disputes should be contemned, so far as either by
inimical or inquisitional influence, they prevent a philosophical

urbanity" (275–276). That time had not yet come for most New Englanders, but in a more practical way Stiles set an example for a remarkable ecumenism within the Christian framework. Before his ordination, Stiles made several trips to Newport, Boston, New York, and Philadelphia where he attended services at Quaker Meetings, Congregational and Episcopal Churches, the Dutch Reformed Church, and the Roman Catholic Church (411). This experience served not only to make him sympathetic to other modes of religious observance (41), but it won for him friends from many Christian denominations, as later his friendly relations with the Jewish religious leaders in Newport made him welcome among the Jews (170–171). It was quite natural that Stiles should take up the cause of Christian Union certainly among all the Congregational churches and among those related by their Calvinistic origin. Holmes quotes his sermon on Christian Union (96–97). For this, again, his contemporaries were not ready.

Holmes' second objective in portraying Stiles is to show him as a dedicated pastor. Throughout his biography he cites examples of his peculiar fitness for his ministerial duties, then gives a long summary, with ample testimony, to illustrate his unusual service to his flock (237–249). Holmes is quite honest in reporting that for his first few years in his Newport church, Stiles preached moral and philosophical sermons, but as soon as his own religious convictions grew more secure and "he was less a Newtonian and more a Christian," he became a zealous preacher of the great truths of the Gospel (238). He thought of himself as being in the apostolic succession and felt it his mission to preach on faith and repentance, Christ's atonement and man's salvation. Holmes quotes from one of Stiles' sermons in which he names the "great truths" that were appropriate for the instruction of the people—"Regeneration, conversion, justification, sanctification and eternal glory," also "the doctrine of the Trinity in Unity, of the divinity and atonement of Christ, with the capital principles of the great theological system of the doctrines of grace" (241). Holmes testifies that Stiles was eloquent and fervent in his

PORTRAIT OF EZRA STILES BY SAMUEL KING, 1771

Yale University Art Gallery

preaching, but as time passed, he became more and more concerned with the poor and uneducated, a fact that was reflected in the simplicity of his sermons which "to the learned were acceptable and improving, to the ignorant they were intelligible, and practically useful" (243).

In a very special way Stiles felt that he was father to his flock. He frequently visited every family, helping and counselling those in need of his advice, adjusting his conversation to their condition, often "borrowing pious instruction from the trees and flowers, from the harvest, from the winds, from the sea, from navigation, manufactures, trade, and commerce" (246). He was particularly sympathetic to children, as he held special services for them and instructed them in private and in gatherings in his own home (246).

Stiles considered himself an evangelist who felt compelled to bring to Christ those who were outside the Church. He had first become interested in missionary work as a young man when, in 1750, he was invited to Stockbridge to preach to the Housatonic Indians. Holmes conjectures that such was Stiles' sympathy and understanding of the people that if his health had permitted him to accept a permanent post there, "he would unquestionably have been an eminent apostle of those American heathen" (20). In Newport, the large group of African slaves gave Stiles an opportunity to win converts to Christ. There were seven Negro communicants in his own church, and he held special meetings to instruct, guide, and counsel them. Many more slaves attended Stiles' church and he baptized many of their children, even though the practice was not generally encouraged in the community. Holmes asks, "If the learned and eminent apostle of the Gentiles appears in the most engaging attitude, while interceding with Philemon, in behalf of his Christian slave, what can exhibit a more interesting spectacle than this Christian pastor, on his knees, surrounded by these Africans, and interceding for them with the God of heaven?" (158)

After twenty years in the ministry, the last of which were spent in virtual exile from his flock when the British invaded

Newport and the inhabitants fled to other communities, Stiles went to Portsmouth where he stayed until he was called to be president of Yale. His extreme reluctance to enter upon an entirely different kind of life, to be separated from his own flock and deprived of his pastoral responsibilities toward them was more than matched by the unwillingness of his people to let him go (248). For years afterward they invited him back, and as he returned he renewed the happy ties that he had earlier enjoyed. Even though at Yale his duties were largely administrative, yet he remained the preacher as he conducted chapel and church services and accepted innumerable invitations to preach from churches throughout New England. In some ways he considered himself a pastor to the students. Holmes says, "To engage the students to a religious life, was, indeed, the object of his assiduous endeavors, and of his constant prayers" (362). All who sought his counsel were tenderly received and given consolation and guidance. If any student fell ill, Stiles visited him immediately to offer the comfort and assistance that a parent would supply.

Holmes concludes his biography with a character sketch of Stiles, stressing particularly his private life (374–378). Here he describes Stiles as a tender husband and an affectionate father, carefully and unfailingly attentive to the intellectual and spiritual improvement of his children. Devout himself, like all clergymen of his time, he maintained a schedule of religious exercises of prayers, hymns, and readings from the Scriptures for the family, morning and evening. According to his biographer, piety and humility and his zeal for imparting to others the divine truths were foremost among his virtues. "If he highly estimated human Learning, he placed a higher estimate on Religion. Living daily under the influence of its precepts; supported through life by its promises; having that hope in death, which it is calculated to inspire; he nobly finished his course, and, with Christian triumph, received the summons to his heavenly mansion" (378).

Abiel Holmes might have written another biography of Stiles as a man of science, for he admits that "with the exception of sacred literature, astronomy was his favorite subject" (354). In describing the portrait of Stiles[10] painted by Samuel King in 1771, Holmes names the books from his library that appear in the background, and they include Newton's *Principia* (153). Also, "At his right hand stands a pillar. On the shaft is a circle, and one trajectory around a solar point, as an emblem of the Newtonian, or Pythagorean, system of the sun, planets, and comets." From Stiles' *Diary* Holmes quotes two passages (66–68) relating to the appearance of a comet in 1744 upon which he had made observations in his sophomore year at college, and another in 1759, which gave him an opportunity to discuss his theories concerning their occurrence. He gives another *Diary* entry for June 3, 1769 which records Stiles' observation of the rare phenomenon of the transit of Venus, which he says will not occur again until A.D. 2004 (134).

In another area of science, Holmes records that on January 1, 1763, upon the receipt of Fahrenheit's thermometer as a gift from Dr. Franklin, Stiles began a series of "thermometrical and meteorological" observations that he continued throughout his life (102–103). Stiles was also interested in American archaeology, particularly in the remains and artifacts of the Indians. Holmes says that he twice examined the puzzling inscription on a rock at Dighton, Massachusetts.[11] He copied the inscription and sent it, along with his own theory that it was Phoenician, to Count de Gebelin of the French Academy who confirmed his hypothesis (119–120). Holmes recalls that when the professor of mathematics and Natural History at Yale resigned his post, Stiles gave the public lectures and also conducted classes as often as possible (279). Although Holmes' own interest was not in science, he appreciated Stiles' achievements and he could have written a very competent sketch of Stiles as an amateur scientist.

As biographer and a Yale man himself, Holmes devoted less attention than one would have expected to the subject of Stiles' presidency of Yale, though, again, the *Diary* contains a great abundance of material. He discusses at length Stiles' hesitation about accepting the post when the offer was extended to him (215–233). His indecision came from his reluctance to leave the life of pastoral duties for the academic world with all of the administrative obligations it carried. Of Stiles' activities after he entered upon his new responsibilities as president, he speaks only in a general way, but he gives an extensive analysis of his intellectual accomplishments. These, he concludes, "joined with his didactic talent, happily qualified him for the office of the presidency" (360). There follows an outline of the subjects he taught the Senior class, his special charge. "He instructed them in metaphysics, ethics, history and civil policy, and in theology" (360). Twice a week he supervised a class in disputation; every week he lectured in Ecclesiastical History. His regular class in Hebrew was not restricted to seniors. At the end of each semester he attended the examinations of all the students. For the daily college chapel service he felt a special responsibility and he normally conducted it unless a visiting clergyman was present. Holmes notes Stiles' often-repeated goal for the college— "I wish to have a virtuous and religious College, as well as a learned one" (363). To insure this end he took pains to know each student, giving special attention to those who had personal problems, illness, financial troubles, or religious doubts. He even undertook the unhappy task of disciplining the unwise or unruly members of the community. Holmes concludes that no president ever served the college with greater fidelity or earned more respect for the institution than Dr. Stiles (370–371).

With the great reservoir of information contained in his *Diary* and the even more valuable testimonia of his vast correspondence, both letters from literary figures and statesmen here and abroad, as well as copies of Stiles' own communications over a long period, Holmes was in an excellent position to write a biography of Stiles' relations with the intellectual and political leaders of his generation. In his treatment of Stiles as a man of religion, Holmes gives some indications of these other roles. He emphasizes his academic attainments, usually calling him "Doctor," as he makes note of the honorary degrees that were conferred upon him: M.A. from Harvard in 1754 (26), D.D. from the University of Edinburgh in 1765 (109), D.D. and LL.D. from Nassau-Hall in New Jersey (later Princeton) in 1779, and D.D. from Dartmouth in 1781 (359–360). The biographer also lists the learned societies to which Stiles had been elected member—the American Philosophical Society, the American Academy of Arts and Sciences, the Connecticut Academy of Arts and Sciences, and the Massachusetts Historical Society (360). Of Stiles' research and historical writings, he mentions two projects, first his *Ecclesiastical History of New-England and of British America* for which he had been collecting material for serveral years and which was begun in 1763. Holmes expresses regret that the confusion of the war and the heavy duties of the presidency of Yale forced Stiles to discontinue the work. He reports that the manuscript is preserved in the cabinet of manuscripts and that he hopes that some day it will be published (132). He gives some interesting information concerning the writing of *A History of Three of the Judges of King Charles I* (321–323). He says that Stiles had been collecting material for this work for many years, but in 1793 a letter from a gentleman from South Carolina written to inquire about the possibility of erecting a monument to the memory of John Dixwell, Esquire, was the stimulus that caused him to finish the work and have it published in 1795. Holmes admires Stiles' reply to a request from a professor in Hamburg for information on the history of Connecticut, for it consisted of eighty-six quarto pages (343–344).

Holmes cites only a very few of the intellectuals among Stiles' friends. The great exception is Benjamin Franklin, in whose honor Stiles delivered a Latin oration at College Hall in 1755 to recognize the scientific discoveries of the eminent scholar. Holmes concludes (27–28), "These two inquisitive and philosophic minds, as if touched at the same instant by the subtil electric fluid, glowed with the ardour of mutual esteem. Their repeated interviews, at this time, cemented a friendship which was never afterward dissolved." He also calls attention to the correspondence between Noah Webster and Stiles (303).

Holmes devoted little attention to Stiles' relations with the other political figures of his day. Aside from noting a visit of President Washington to New Haven in 1789 and an interview with him in New York (308), the ceremony of conferring an honorary degree upon John Adams in 1788 (304), and a visit to his long-time friend, Governor Jonathan Trumbull (221), he mentions few of the men who were making history at that momentous time. Even the sufferings and great dislocations experienced first by his parish in Newport when the town was occupied by the British (200–201), and then by Yale College when the enemy troops entered New Haven harbor and took over the town (261–265) are minimized, though Holmes was in possession of plenty of material on these events.[12] Instead, in speaking about the war, he dwells upon Stiles' attitude toward the position of the States in relation to England, his ideas on liberty, and his strong support of the final struggle for independence (210–213). Most impressive is Holmes' account of the "Election Sermon" preached on May 8, 1783, at the request of Governor Trumbull, to mark the cessation of hostilities and the beginning of the independent government of the United States (282–286).

Because Abiel Holmes lived in an era that had attitudes and values different from our own, in all probability he would not have accepted our suggestions for a full account of the life of Ezra Stiles. Rather, like Izaak Walton who depicted George Herbert in his life of the poet "like a Saint, unspotted by the World, full of Alms-deeds, full of Humility, and all the examples of a vertuous life,"[13] Holmes endeavored to portray Stiles as a saintly man and a zealous Christian. In summing up the contributions of a remarkable scholar, minister, and college president, he says, "Piety, like a golden chain, has served, at once, to give a connexion and ornament to the work, which the assemblage of genius, learning, and the most refined morality, could never have furnished.—A Christian believer on unshakable principles, he gloried in nothing so much as in the cross of Christ, and next to his own immortal interest, his zeal and talents were unitedly employed, to bring others to the saving knowledge of divine truth." (377–378).

A Family Tablet

In his *Life of Ezra Stiles*, Abiel Holmes recounts at length an episode that occurred in 1786, when, during the course of the autumn vacation from college President Stiles made a journey to New York State and Vermont to examine the battlefields of the Revolution.[1] Shortly after starting out, Stiles met with a young man whom Holmes identifies only as a former student at Yale, an orphan, "a youth of fine genius," who had enjoyed the president's patronage at college. This was St. John Honeywood, valedictorian of his class of 1782,[2] and a great favorite in the Stiles' household. Honeywood was so delighted to be of some small service as companion to his admired preceptor, and to share his appreciation of the beautiful northern autumn, that he wrote the details in a letter to Holmes. In it, he tells, for example, of examining a giant tree that had been felled recently and finding two hundred forty growth rings, and again, of the incomparable view of the Green Mountains from Bennington. He drew a sketch of the mountains and sent it to Holmes along

with a poem he composed to express in verse the president's
poetic comparison of the landscape to that of Palestine (which he
had never seen). Because it is so typical of the religious verse that
was being written in America at the end of the eighteenth
century, I shall quote it entirely:

> "Tis thus, (he cried) as hushed in soft repose,
> On Zion's plains the sacred Jordan flows;
> Thus rise his banks, with palms and willows crown'd,
> Where Salem's virgins, to the silver sound
> Of mystic cymbals, danc'd. On every side,
> Thus Juda's mountains rise, in airy pride.
> Thus Olivet, where erst th' incarnate God,
> Retiring with his faithful followers, trod—
> Whence, as in dazzling majesty, he rose,
> He saw the sapphire gates of heaven unclose
> Wrapp'd in effulgence, met the angelic throng,
> And heard their lyre awake the victor song.[3]

This talented young man, St. John Honeywood, was born in
Leicester, Massachusetts in 1764, the son of a physician. Early
left an orphan, he was sent to Lebanon, Connecticut, for his pre-
college education. Soon after his matriculation at Yale in 1778,
"he became the distinguished favorite of the President, Dr.
Stiles, into whose house, during his residence in New Haven, he
was received with parental kindness."[4] After graduation, he
spent two years in Schenectady as a master in an academy, then
at Albany he studied law and was admitted to the bar. He
practiced law in Salem for ten years before entering state politics.
All his life Honeywood enjoyed sketching and painting. It is said
that "his favorite style was caricature, and he would have been
no unsuccessful imitator of Hogarth."[5] He was also interested in
writing poetry. In 1801, three years after his untimely death, a
volume of his poems was published by an anonymous editor
through the subscription of a large group of friends.

During his college years, 1778–1782, St. John Honeywood
was a frequent caller at the home of President Stiles, where he
enjoyed the learned conversation of the great man, but the

DRAWING OF THE STILES FAMILY BY ST. JOHN HONEYWOOD

Beinecke Rare Book and Manuscript Library, Yale University

society of the five Stiles daughters provided more entertainment. He wrote verses to the girls and drew sketches for them. Fortunately, one of these which he drew of the whole family, on a page of the president's *Diary*, has been preserved.[6] Although in the drawing none of the girls is beautiful, they had other graces, notably liveliness and wit, that charmed the artist. He liked all of them, but he was especially attracted to Elizabeth whom he asked, in vain, to marry him. At this time six Stiles children were at home—Elizabeth, Kezia Taylor, Emilia, Ruth, Mary, and one of the sons, Isaac. All of them welcomed the society of the Yale students, particularly St. John Honeywood and Abiel Holmes. In the absence of musical instruments in that Puritan household, they often amused themselves during the long winter evenings in singing and improvising poetry. At all events, it seems to have been an especially happy time for the family and the students.

In 1796, just fourteen years after Honeywood's graduation, only two of the Stiles children were living—Emilia married that same year to Jonathan Leavitt, a lawyer in Greenfield, Massachusetts, and Ruth who later (1799) married the Reverend Caleb Gannett of Cambridge. Ezra, Jr., who had married Sibyl Avery in 1781 and had two children, died in 1784. His brother Isaac was lost at sea in 1795. Kezia Taylor, who married Lewis Burr Sturges, died in 1785; Mary, who in 1790 had married the Reverend Abiel Holmes, died in 1795, the same year as her sister, Elizabeth, who had not married. In order to make some fitting memorial to his friends of happier days and to preserve their poetry, Abiel Holmes edited a small volume which he called *A Family Tablet*, and had it published in Boston in 1796, but as editor he remained anonymous and all of the poems are followed by pseudonyms, with the exception of two signed "St. John" (Honeywood).

A Family Tablet contains forty-six poems, of which twelve are elegies or dirges, four hymns, several poetic epistles, and the rest what might be called occasional poems. Seventeen are signed by Myron (Abiel Holmes), twelve by Louisa (Emilia), seven by

Myra (Mary), three by Eugenio (Ezra, Jr.), three by Cecelia (unidentified), two by St. John (Honeywood), and one each by Henry and Narcissa (both unidentified). The names were not arbitrarily assigned by Holmes, for they occur in the text of many of the poems and appear to be the private names by which these close friends addressed one another.

Holmes must have realized that the poems have no literary value, for in his preface he tries to discourage "the hand of Criticism" by expressing his confidence that "the eye of Friendship, for which it is immediately designed, will assuredly peruse it with indulgence. If the partiality of Affection has given it an undue estimation, Candour will draw her veil over the venial error." [7] The first poems, as one might expect, are concerned with the unhappy events of the years immediately preceding the publication, when so many deaths broke up the family circle forever. It opens with an elegy written by Louisa, to mourn the deaths of her father, Dr. Stiles, and her sister, Mary Holmes, in 1795. Two excerpts will serve to convey the general tone and character of this poem and the other dirges:

> A distant gale the solemn curfew bears,
>   And death-like murmurs on its pinions ride;
> Ah Frantic sound! the mouldering urn receives
>   My aged Sire, my life, my joy, my pride.

> Scarce had the curfew's sad vibrations ceas'd,
>   Ere death's stern mandate bids it strike anew;
> Near and more near the hollow notes prevail,
>   Where lov'd Maria breathes her last adieu.

In another elegy, "Lines addressed to Miss S.W., on the death of her brother," Louisa pays tribute to the memory of her deceased brother, Ezra, and her sister, Kezia. Two separate elegies are devoted to these two members of the family. Cecelia writes an "Elegiac Fragment on the death of E.S., Esq, who died in North-Carolina" and Myron writes an "Elegiac Sonnet on Mrs. K.T.S. who died within a year after her marriage." Another family elegy is written by Myron, "Elegy on Doctor ******," his father, who had been a surgeon in the army. A "Dirge" on the death of young Henry, by Myra, suggests that Henry was also one of the family group, but he has not been identified. There are also a number of other elegiac poems paying tribute to various friends, including one to the parents of a young man who was lost at sea, and one "On the sudden death of a lovely child."

Another group of poems, also in a serious vein, comprises several hymns, of which two written by the clergyman, Myron, are noteworthy: "Hymn written at sea" and "Hymn" based upon Ps. 30:15. Only a few of the poems were inspired by recollections of the Revolution. Two of these are the work of Eugenio, the only one of the family circle who was old enough to have experienced the real tragedy of war as he fought the British troops invading New Haven in 1779. In one poem, "Lines occasioned by the war, 1777," he says that he must abandon the poetry of nature and peace to tell of the horrors of war which threaten Liberty herself in his country. In the other, "Andre's ghost," Major Andre's spirit comes back from heaven to comfort his sister and to predict an inglorious end for Arnold who betrayed him, his friend. A third poem by St. John, entitled "The soldier," is a more academic piece in which a soldier tells his friend that he was forced to go into the war because he was rejected by his Julia. Shortly after, he is felled by an enemy bullet.

But the book also contains many poems that come from a happier time in the lives of the Stiles family, when they were in New Haven, enjoying the pleasant association with Yale students. These range from an "Address to a young robin which flew into my window," by Myra, and an equally guileless one by Louisa called "Lines (accompanying a needle-book) addressed to Rozella, a very small but beautiful doll of my little friend, Miss A.P.," to an elaborate mock-serious poem full of classical allusions, called "Transformation of Eliza into a poplar," by Myron. Some are gay, light-hearted trifles directed to one or another of the group on some slight pretext, intended apparently

solely for the momentary amusement of the recipient. The only
one that seems pretentious is entitled "Yaratildia, an epic poem,"
by Myron, on a tiresome experience of his wife in spinning yarn
and knitting stockings.[8]

From the collection three poems stand out as being most
successful in conveying to another age the mentality and character of a special group of people. They are two love poems, one
written by Myra and the answer by Myron, shortly before their
marriage, then an epilogue by St. John. The editor supplies the
background, with dates. When Myron was in South Carolina in
1784, he sent some jonquil bulbs back to Connecticut. There
was, however, some mishap with the shipment and so he
concluded that they were lost. Then, in 1787, he received from
Myra a poem entitled "To Myron, with a jonquil." With charm
and delicacy she bids the jonquil go to Myron:

> Go, happy flower! to Myron's chamber fly,
> Bloom in his presence, in his absence die.

Myron's acknowledgement in his poem "Reply" is equally
successful in expressing his love for Myra:

> Sweet lovely flower! by that fair Nymph caress'd,
> Myron thrice welcome hails thee to his breast.
> Here all thy verdure, all they sweets display,
> Bloom while she smiles and when she frowns, decay.

Honeywood, upon reading the two poems some time later, and
contrasting his own unhappy lot of having his love rejected by
Elizabeth, and knowing that all the pleasant companionship with
the Stileses and their friends had been lost, wrote a poem entitled
"On reading the above piece." Sadly he asks to have the memory
of those joyous days erased from his mind.

> Gentlest Nymph! whose fairy hand
> Taught the Jonquil to grow,

> To me that generous aid impart;
> On me exert that magic power,
> Tear each fond image from my heart,
> Bid me forget each happier hour.

   May I forget thy welcome home,
      And all the once-loved charms of Yale!

So it was that, by an ironical turn of events, Honeywood, who
had done more than most students to secure bright college years
for himself and his friends, came in the end to wish only to efface
every recollection of his days at Yale.[9]

HUMPHREYS PRESENTING TO CONGRESS COLORS CAPTURED AT YORKTOWN. By an unidentified artist

Colonel David Humphreys
and the Stiles Family

ON DECEMBER 8, 1781, President Ezra Stiles of Yale entrusted to the care of Colonel David Humphreys to be delivered to General Washington a tin case containing a diploma as testimony of the conferring of the honorary degree of Doctor of Laws upon the general. A covering letter repeated the Yale citation of Washington's achievements as "the Deliverer of your Country, the Defender of the Liberty and Rights of humanity, and the Maecenas of Science and Literature." [1] No more fitting person could have been found to carry out this mission than Colonel Humphreys, one of the most loyal of patriots and the devoted friend of Washington [2] for whom he had served as aide-de-camp during the war.

David Humphreys (1752–1818) [3] distinguished himself in his long service to his country, first in the army and later in Europe, as a diplomat. He was born in Derby, Connecticut, the son of the Reverend Daniel Humphreys, a Congregational minister, and was educated at Yale, receiving a bachelor's degree in 1771 and a master's degree in 1774. During his years at college he was particularly interested in literature; he was one of the earliest members of the prestigious Brothers in Unity society, and he counted Timothy Dwight as one of his best friends. He was offered a post as tutor at Yale, but he felt obliged to decline it in order to join the army. In the military service he had a brilliant career, attaining the rank of brigadier-colonel at the age of twenty-eight. He served successively as aide-de-camp to Generals Putnam, Greene, and Washington, and saw action in the major engagements in New York and New Jersey. The most dramatic event in his service came after the surrender of the British at Yorktown when he was sent to Philadelphia to present the captured standards of Lord Cornwallis to the Congress assembled in that city. The splendid hero's welcome that he received is depicted in a painting now in the New Haven Colony Historical Society.[4]

After the war, Colonel Humphreys spent some time with Washington as he undertook the great task of restoring the arts of peace. In 1784 he was sent to France and England as secretary to a Commission empowered to negotiate treaties for trade and commerce. Returning for a short stay in America, he was elected a member of the Assembly of Connecticut. In 1790 he was appointed to the important post of Minister to Portugal and then to Spain, where he performed distinguished service in gaining respect for his country and favorable conditions for her commerce. When he came back to America, he immediately turned his attention to the improvement of American agriculture and to the stimulation of industry. To this end he introduced the raising of merino sheep imported from Spain, and built factories for the manufacture of fine woolen goods in the state.

One of the Connecticut Wits, Humphreys had written both poetry and prose since his college days. His *Essay on the Life of the Honorable Major-General Israel Putnam* is a valuable record since it was based to a large extent upon his acquaintance with the General as he served under him during the war. In poetry, besides a number of experimental poems in classical forms, he wrote two long narrative works in heroic couplets, both designed to inspire in his fellow-countrymen his own hopes for the future of America. They are: *A Poem Addressed to the Armies of the United States of America* (1780) and *A Poem on the Happiness of America: Addressed to the Citizens of the United States of America* (1786).

There had been a long association between the Humphreys and the Stiles families. In his *Diary* Ezra Stiles records that his father, the Reverend Isaac Stiles, officiated at the ordination of the father of Colonel Humphreys, the Reverend Daniel Humphreys on May 6, 1734 and preached the Ordination Sermon. (I.128) In the course of his life-long service to the Church in Derby, the Reverend Daniel Humphreys kept in touch with the Stiles family, for Stiles records at least three instances when he preached all day for "good Mr. Humphrey." (II.305, 368, 502) So it seems quite natural that when the minister died on September 2, 1789, at the age of eighty-one, Ezra Stiles attended the funeral and, at the request of Humphreys' son, delivered a eulogy. (III.281)

President Stiles' relations with Colonel Humphreys may be judged by a number of entries in the *Diary* which give an impression of their common concern with the war, the restoration of the country, the government, and the establishment of sound relations with Europe. There is, for example, an unusually interesting note of December 6, 1781, where he says, "Spent the Evening with Colonel Humphrey aid de Camp to his Excellency G. Washington, who gave an Account of the Siege and Capture of Lord Cornwallis, he having been present through the whole. He corrected my Plan." Immediately before this entry Stiles had sketched his version of the plan of the battle of Yorktown, then, immediately after, he drew a revised plan according to Humphreys' information. (II.569–570)

During the years following the war, Stiles records a number of visits to him in New Haven. On June 8, 1784, Governor Jefferson of Virginia and with him General Humphreys visited him when they were on their way to survey the Eastern States.

(III.124) On June 6, 1786, a simple entry records that Colonel Humphreys passed through Town to Hartford. (III.220) The following year, February 3, 1787, he notes that Emilia, his daughter, went to Hartford with Colonel Humphreys. (III.254) On the first of May of that year Stiles notes that Colonel Humphreys left New Haven for the general meeting in Philadelphia of the Connecticut Society of the Cincinnati. (III.260) A week later he reports the receipt of two volumes of the *American Travels* of the Marquis de Chastellux sent to him by Humphreys. (III.262) In 1789 and 1790, Stiles notes four more occasions when Humphreys was in New Haven and visited him. (III.260, 364, 371, 555) On July 10, 1789 he notes that his daughter, Emilia, and a Mrs. Wyllis sailed for New York with the colonel. (III.316) While Humphreys was serving on diplomatic missions to Europe, he wrote to Stiles and had in return a number of letters from him, several of which were delivered by Stiles' son, Isaac, who made several trips abroad during that time. One entry in his *Diary*, dated April 6, 1792, reads: "By him (son Isaac) I received a Letter dated Lisbon 14 February from his excellency Colonel Humphreys Ambassador from Congress to the Court of Portugal in which he gives me an account of the State of Literature in Portugal." (III.447)[5]

A pleasing memento of the happy relationship between the Stiles family and Humphreys is preserved in a copy of his *Miscellaneous Works*, published by Hodge, Allen, and Campbell (N.Y., 1790), which he presented to one of Ezra Stiles' daughters. An inscription on the flyleaf reads: "Presented to Miss Amelia Stiles[6] by the Author—the Minister of the United States to her serene Majesty the Queen of Portugal." Affixed below is the bookplate of Jonathan Leavitt, Jr., who married Amelia in 1796. The book had been treasured by five generations of the descendants of the couple, and was lately in the library of Dr. Charles J. Foote of New Haven.

As there are only a few copies of this book in the United States, and as a later edition published in 1804[7] soon replaced the first, it is worthwhile to examine this volume. Obviously the author had given considerable thought to selecting the contents, and to presenting them in such a way that they would appeal to both his American and his European readers. The book is dated July 4, 1790, and is dedicated to the noted French reformer, the Duc de la Rochefoucault, whom he had met in Paris, and whom he describes as "So able a defender of the rights of human nature." Humphreys then presented several testimonials to his writings: extracts from Joel Barlow's *Vision of Columbus* (1787), from the *Critical Review* (June, 1785), from the *Monthly Review* (May, 1785), from the *Journal de Paris* (May 7, 1786), and from an English translation of the introductory letter prefixed by the Marquis de Chastellux to his own French translation of Humphreys' *Address to the Armies*.

Perhaps because Humphreys considered his two long heroic poems his most significant works, he begins the volume with his *Address to the Armies* and his *Poem on the Happiness of America*. The first had earlier been printed in New Haven, in London, and in Paris and won great acclaim for the author in England as well as in France.[8] The other, longer (1095 lines) poem was published first in London and then in Hartford. It too, was lauded for its inspirational message both at home and abroad. There follows a series of shorter poems, chiefly on classical models, including an elegy, an epistle, an epithalamium, a fable, and an epitaph, mostly dealing with contemporary situations. This section also includes (odd though it may strike us) Dryden's *Alexander's Feast* and an *Epistle* from Timothy Dwight in answer to one addressed to him by Humphreys. Finally, there is his earliest published poem, an *Elegy on the Burning of Fairfield in Connecticut*, "written in 1779, on the Spot where the Town stood." The next section is occupied by a long tragedy entitled *The Widow of Malabar or The Tyranny of Custom* which Humphreys says is imitated from the French of the contemporary tragic poet, M. LeMierre. It is preceded by a dedicatory epistle to John Trumbull, Esq. who collaborated with Humphreys in writing the Prologue and the Epilogue. There is also a cast of characters who presented the play in Philadelphia on May 7, 1790. This is followed by a Prologue and an Epilogue to the translation of Racine's tradedy *Athaliah*. Finally, there is Timothy Dwight's *Ode on the Glory of Columbia*. The last section has Humphreys' long *Essay on the Life of the Honorable Major-General Israel Putnam* which the author claims is the first biography written on this continent. Prepared at the invitation of the Connecticut Society of the Cincinnati, it was dedicated to the president of that organization of the veterans of the war, Colonel Jeremiah Wadsworth. The final item is Humphreys' *An Oration on the Political Situation of the United States of America in the Year 1789* which was "Pronounced before the State Society of the Cincinnati of Connecticut, at New Haven, in Celebration of the Thirteenth Anniversary of Independence."

The time and care that Humphreys expended upon the preparation of his volume of *Miscellaneous Works* gives some indication of the fact that, though he was primarily a man of action—soldier, diplomat, industrialist, and farmer—he was also keenly interested in literature. He speaks of this to his old friend, John Trumbull, in the dedication of his *Widow of Malabar*, where he says, "Had not the tumultuous scenes, which commenced with the late war, separated our little society, we might perhaps have innocently indulged ourselves considerably more in literary speculations, than the circumstances have since permitted."[9] In Humphreys' literary activities, as in so many other aspects of his life, Ezra Stiles played a part. His biographer reports that in 1778, when Colonel Humphreys was revising his first draft of the *Address to the American Armies*, he solicited the criticism of his scholarly friends, among whom was President Ezra Stiles.[10] In a letter to General Greene (April 10, 1780), Humphreys gives a playful explanation for his own writing: "Now what could induce me to turn Scribbler, whether my own sins or those of my Parents (as Pope says) must be left to further discussion; tho I rather imagine the mischief, like a thousand others, will be found to have originated in a great measure, from keeping ill Company, such as the before mentioned Colonel Wadsworth, a certain Mr. Trumbull, a Mr. Dwight, a Dr. Stiles and some other similar characters of smaller notoriety. These men are enough to corrupt half of the youth of the State, and introduce them to the same evil practices." [11]

Notes

Notes to The Oldest Library Motto

1. The exhibition is fully described and illustrated in the catalogue *Ramsès le Grand* (Paris, 1976).

2. The *New York Times* for 14 November 1976, gives an account of the problem.

3. *Biblioteca historica* I.47–49, ed. C.H. Oldfather (London, 1935), I.166–175.

4. Cicero, *Acad.* 2.127; *Tusc. Dis.*, 5.69 and 3.1.

5. *Epistola ad Guarinum suum Veronesem*, 18 January 1417.

6. Johannes Duft, *Die Stiftsbibliothek Sankt Gallen: Der Barocksaal und seine Putten* (St. Gall, 1974) p. 13.

7. Justus Lipsius, *De Bibliothecis Syntagma* (Antwerp, 1706) p. 9.

8. This is quoted by E. Stickelberger, "Ein Philobiblon aus der Barockzeit," in *Stultifera Navia* 14 (1957), p. 100, and there is a facsimile of the title page on p. 135.

9. A facsimile of the title page is reproduced in I. Odelstierna, "ΨΥΧΗΣ IATPEION" in *Donum Grapeanum: Festschrift Tillägnad Anders Grape* (Upsala, 1945), p. 398.

10. Horace, *Odes* III.1.1–2; Virgil, *Aeneid* VI.250.

11. I.Odelstierna, *Donum Grapeanum*, pp. 376–378.

12. J.Duft, *Die Stiftsbibliothek Sankt Gallen*, 7–15.

13. There is a photograph in Duft, p. 12.

14. In 1764 the motto was used over the portal of the ducal library of Modena. (P. Scherrer, "Bibliotheken und Bibliothekare als Träger kultureller Aufgaben," *Nachrichten der Vereinigung Schweitzerischer Bibliothekare* 32 (1956), p. 131.

Notes to The Clock of Eternal Wisdom

1. Aulus Gellius, *Noctes Atticae, Praefatio* (ed. J.C. Rolfe, Cambridge, 1946), p. xxix.

2. *Aurora Petri Rigae Versificata, Praefatio*, ed. P. Beichner (Notre Dame, 1965), pp. 7–8.

3. Modern edition of P. Mons (Trier, 1968).

4. Ibid., "Vorspruch," p. 23.

5. Ibid., "Vorspruch," p. 26.

6. Ibid., "Der dritter Teil," p. 162.

7. Ed. J. Strange (Cologne, 1861), "Prologus," pp. 9–10.

8. Ibid., Book III, chap. 6, p. 210.

9. D. Planzer, "Das Horologium sapientiae des Heinrich Suso, O.P." *Divus Thomas*, Freiburg, XII (1934), p. 130.

10. J.A. Bizet, *Henri Suso et le déclin de la scolastique* (Paris, 1946), pp. 55–71.

11. *Heinrich Suso: Studien zum 600 Todestag, 1366–1966*, ed. E.M. Filthaut (Cologne, 1966).

12. Ibid., pp. 161–165.

13. Ms. IV.III. See E.P. Spencer, "L'Horloge de Sapience," *Scriptorium*, XVII (1933), pp. 277–299.

14. *Heinrich Suso: Studien*, pp. 319–337.

15. Ibid., pp. 345–359.

16. Ibid., pp. 408–419.

Note: A reproduction, in color, of the miniature of the clock in a fifteenth-century French manuscript is printed in *Smithsonian* IX, no. 7 (1978), pp. 114–115.

Notes to The Mystical Symbol of the Beryl

1. Karl Bormann, "Eine bisher verschollene Handschrift von De beryllo," *Mitteilungen und Forschungsbeiträge des Cusanus-Gesellschaft* X (1973), 104–105.

2. L. Baur ed. *Nicolai de Cusa De Beryllo* (Leipzig, 1940) ix–xiii.

3. Bormann, "Eine bisher verschollene Handschift", 105.

4. E. Vansteenberghe, *Le Cardinal Nicolas de Cusa* (Paris, 1920) 272, 273, 482.

5. *Liber lapidum* XII (ed. P. Ropartz, p. 138) where he credits the beryl with curative powers for diseases of the eyes and the liver.

6. *De lapidibus* 2, cap. 2 (ed. A. Borgnet, V.32) follows Marbode.

7. K. Fleischmann, *Nikolaus von Cues Über den Beryll* (Leipzig, 1938) 134, note 6.

8. "et per ipsum videns attingit prius invisibile." (*De beryllo* II, ed. Baur, p. 4).

9. "Intellectualibus oculis si intellectualis beryllus, qui formam habeat maximam pariter et minimam, adaptatur, per eius medium attingitur indivisibile omnium principium." (ed. Baur, pp. 4–5).

Notes to The Symbol of the Y

1. The most complete treatment of the subject is that of S.C. Chew in *The Pilgrimage of Life* (New Haven, 1962).

2. Lactantius, the fourth-century Christian apologist, however, found the idea of the two ways incompatible with orthodox theology. See *Divinarum institutionum libri septem* VI.3.1–5, ed. S. Brandt, *Corpus scriptorum ecclesiasticorum* XIX, p. 485.

3. The best modern discussion of the theme is given by E. Panofsky in *Hercules am Scheidewege* (Leipzig, 1930).

4. I have discussed the history of the text in "Aesticampianus' Edition of the *Tabula* Attributed to Cebes," in *Essays on Manuscripts and Rare Books* (Hamden, 1975), pp. 79–86.

5. The history of the use of the symbol is traced by Wolfgang Harms in *Homo viator in bivio. Studien zur Bildlichkeit des Weges* (Munich, 1970).

6. The chief witness to the use of the letter in the East is an impressive relief on the tombstone of a Neopythagorean of the first century of our era. The stone slab, found in Lydia, has a very large letter Y carved upon it. See A. Brinkmann, "Ein Denkmal des Neupythagoreismus," *Rheinisches Museum für Philologie* (1911), pp. 616–625.

7. Satire III,56–57, Satire V,34–35. See T.E. Mommsen, "Petrarch and the Story of the Choice of Hercules," *Journal of the Warburg and Courtauld Institutes* XVI (1953), pp. 183–188.

8. *Aeneid* VI,542–543.

9. See A. Dimier, "La lettre de Pythagore et les Hagiographes du Moyen Age," *Le Moyen Age* IX (1954), pp. 403–418, and H. Silvestre, "Nouveaux témoignages médiévaux de la 'littera Pythagorae'," *Le Moyen Age* XXVIII (1973), pp. 201–207.

10. For an account of the school, see E. Lesne, *Histoire de la Propriété ecclésiastique en France* (Lille, 1940), V Les écoles, pp. 96–101.

11. Ibid., 101–102; M.L. Laistner, *Thought and Letters in Western Europe 600–900* (N.Y., 1930), pp. 210–211; M. Manitius, *Geschichte der lateinischen Literatur des Mittelalters* (Munich, 1911), II,807–808.

12. For a discussion of Remigius, see M.Manitius, *Geshichte der lateinischen Literatur*, I,504–519; *Remigius Autissiodorensis Commentum in Martianum Capellam*, ed. C.E. Lutz (Leyden, 1962), I,5–16.

13. *In Aeneidem*, VI,136 (ed. G. Thilo, Leipzig, 1887, II,30–31).

14. *De Nuptiis Philologiae et Mercurii*, II.102 (ed. A. Dick, Leipzig, 1925, p. 43, 16–18).

15. *Etymologiae*, I.2.7 (ed. W.M. Lindsay, Oxford, 1911).

16. See J.P. Elder, "A Mediaeval Cornutus on Persius," *Speculum* XX (1944), p. 246.

17. *Auli Persii Flacci Satirarum Liber*, Scholia ad III,56 (ed. O. Jahn, Leipzig, 1843, p. 302).

18. *Poetae latini aevi Carolini* III,12, *Heirici carmina vitae S. Germani* I, lines 78–84, ed. L. Traube (Berlin, 1896), pp. 440–441.

19. M. Manitius, "Remigiusscholien," *Münchener Museum* III (1913), p. 100.

20. Ibid.

21. *Commentum in Martianum Capellam* II,43,18, ed. C.E. Lutz, I. p. 147.

22. J. Conington, *The Satires of A. Persius Flaccus* (Oxford, 1893), p. 61.

23. *Lives of the Eminent Philosophers* VIII, ed. R.D. Hicks (London, 1931), II pp. 320–366.

24. *Works and Days*, 287–292, ed. H.G. Evelyn-White (Cambridge, 1936), p. 25.

25. W. Harms, *Homo viator in bivio*, has reproduced a large number of these. See Plates 1–49.

26. *Champfleury* (Paris, 1529) p. LXIII[r.]

27. *Emblemata* (Amsterdam, 1625), pt. 2, p.49.

28. The simplest explanation would be that by an engraver's error the whole scene was presented in reverse.

Notes to The Letter of Lentulus

1. See E. von Dobschütz, "Christusbilder," in *Texte und Untersuchungen zur Geschichte der altchristlichen Literatur*, XVIII (1899), p. 308.

2. See Laurentius Valla, *De falso credita et ementita Constantini donatione declamatio*, ed. W. Schwahn (Leipzig, 1928), p. 62.

3. See the edition of Basel, 1562–1569, vol. I, p. 554: "Lentuli epistola ad imperatorem Tiberium quae apud Eutropium in annalibus senatorum Romanorum extat."

4. The British Museum *Catalogue* lists seven editions published in the nineteenth century.

5. See M.R. James, *The Apocryphal New Testament* (Oxford, 1924), pp. 477–478. Modern scholars note three main points where the letter violates historicity: (1) there was no Publius Lentulus, governor of Judea, preceding Pontius Pilate; (2) if there had been a procurator of Syria, he would have written to the Emperor, not the Senate, for the province was an imperial one; and (3) the title Jesus Christus was not used as early as this.

6. Ioh. Christoph. Mylius, in his catalogue, *Memorabilia Bibliothecae Academiae Ienensis* (Jena, 1746), describes two manuscripts that contain the letter. The first, N.B.[1], a sixteenth-century manuscript that has an unusually fine representation of Christ on the cover, contains the Lentulus letter along with some theological texts. The second, N.B. 80, written in the sixteenth century, records the letter as Item 11, and gives the explicit (see p. 347).

7. Nicephorus Callistus, *Ecclesiastica Historia*, I.40 (P.G., CXLV.748–750).

8. For the French translation by P. Durand, see M. Didron, *Manual d'iconographie chrétienne* (Paris, 1845), p. 452.

9. Johannes Damascenus, *Epistola ad Theophilum imperatorem de sanctis et venerandis imaginibus* (P.G., XCV.349).

10. F. Vigouroux, *Dictionnaire de la Bible* (Paris, 1908), IV.171, says without reservation that the Lentulus letter must come from the same source as the three other descriptions. F.X. Kraus, in *Real-Encyclopädie der christlichen Altertums* (Freiburg, 1882), II.15–16, expresses complete agreement.

11. P.G., XCIV.1262.

12. For a discussion of the portrait in Edessa, see W.Grimm, "Die Sage vom Ursprung der Christusbilder" in *Kleinere Schriften* (Berlin, 1883), pp. 166–173.

13. See Eusebius Caesarensis, *Historia ecclesiastica, Latine Rufino Aquileiensi interprete* (Utrecht, 1474), I, cap. XVI–XVIII.

14. See L.J. Tixeront, *Les origines de l'église d'Edessa et la légende d'Abgar* (Paris, 1888).

15. Like the Veronica legend, the tradition of the miraculous portrait becomes diffused in the West. For the disputed location of the original, see W. Grimm, "Die Sage vom Ursprung der Christusbilder", pp. 171–173.

16. IV.26–27 (*P.G., LXXXVI.2716*).

17. See J.D. Mansi, *Sacrorum Conciliorum nova collectio* (Florence, 1766), XII.963–964.

18. See F. Combefis, *Originum rerumque Constantinopolitanarum manipulus* (Paris, 1664), pp. 75–101, "Constantini Porphyrogennetae: Narratio de divina Christi Dei nostri imagine non manufacta."

19. XVI. cap. 25 (*P.G.*, CXXXV.118–119).

20. Didron, *Manual d'iconographie chrétienne*, p. 12.

21. Ibid., p. 15.

Notes to The "Gentle Puritan"

1. *The Literary Diary of Ezra Stiles, D.D., LL.D.* ed. F.B. Dexter (New York, 1901), III.502–503. For bibliographical details concerning Stiles I am indebted to Edmund Morgan's *The Gentle Puritan* (New Haven, 1962).

2. The manuscript (now MS. 27 in the Beinecke Library) was described by Thomas E. Marston in the *Gazette* for January 1968. (The Stiles notation appears on the *verso* of leaf 90.)

3. Anne S. Pratt, "The Books Sent from England by Jeremiah Dummer to Yale College," in *Papers in Honor of Andrew Keogh* (New Haven, 1938), p. 436. The identification with the *Speculum humanae salvationis* was based on Ezra Stiles' annotation.

4. A few manuscripts have an interpolation in the "Prohemium" giving the date as 1324. It has been conjectured that the author was Ludolph of Saxony. M.R. James in his *Speculum humanae salvationis* (Oxford, 1926), analyzes the treatise and gives the history of the text.

5. James, *Speculum humanae salvationis*, p. 6.

6. *Diary*, III.481.

7. *Diary*, III.400 (1 August, 1790).

8. Quoted by Morgan, *The Gentle Puritan*, p. 72.

9. *Diary*, III.275 (10 August 1787). Stiles mentions his reading of Aquinas also in the *Diary*, III.116.

Notes to *A Forged Manuscript in Boustrophedon*

1. *Corpus Inscriptionum Graecarum*, I.i, pp. 15 ff. Also in England, in Wilton House, Wiltshire, there is a fine example of boustrophedon on a marble votive relief dedicated to Zeus.

2. George Herbert's "Easter Wings," and "Altar" have made the figure-poem familiar to English readers.

3. A.N.L. Munby, in his *Portrait of an Obsession* (New York, 1967), pp. 202–217, gives a full account of Simonides' transactions in England.

4. Numbers 13879, 13880, 13881, 13892, and 13877 in the *Catalogue of the Phillipps Collection*.

5. Munby, *Portrait of an Obsession*, 202.

6. Quoted in *Phillipps Catalogue*, p. 255.

7. Elegies 1, 3, 5, and 6 of the traditional editions.

8. These poems, for which the ultimate source is the *Palatine Anthology*, have been edited by U. de Wilamowitz-Moellendorf in *Bucolici Graeci* (Oxford, 1910), pp. 140–154.

9. Brunck, R.J.P., ed., *Analecta veterum poetarum Graecorum* (Strassburg, 1876), II,292–293, and III.327.

Notes to *Copernicus' Stand for Humanism*

1. Edited by R. Hercher, *Epistolographi Graeci* (Paris, 1873), 767–786, with the title: *Theophylacti Simocati Scholastici Epistolae morales rusticae amatoriae*.

2. Cracow, 1509.

3. The five known extant copies are all in libraries in eastern Europe.

4. *Teofilakt Symokatta Listy* ed. R. Gansiniec (Wroclaw, 1953).

5. The letter (*Praefatio*) is printed in the modern edition of F. and C. Zeller (Munich, 1949), vol. II, pp. 30–31. The letter is very pertinent to the situation in which Copernicus found himself. In order to avoid having his work fall into the hands of ignorant or malicious people who would distort it, he delayed the publication of his great masterpiece for thirty-six years.

6. See L. Prowe, *Nicolaus Coppernicus* (Berlin, 1883) I.2, pp. 375–377. Joannes Dantiscus, the poet laureate, was a good friend of Copernicus, and in 1541 wrote a Latin epigram for Copernicus' *De lateribus et angulis triangulorum*. See Ioannis Dantisci *Carmina*, ed. S. Skamina (Cracow, 1950) pp. 209–210.

7. Besides books on astronomy, mathematics, and physics, the list includes ancient philosophers, historians, and poets, along with a few works by Italian humanists like Pico della Mirandola and Lorenzo Valla.

8. The best account of this phenomenon can be found in M. Bogucka, *Nicholas Copernicus. The Country and Times*, tr. by L. Szwaicer (Wroclaw, 1973), pp. 52–58.

9. *De revolutionibus*, Proemium. Ed. Zeller, vol II, pp. 8–9.

Notes to *A Roman Proverb*

1. Book XVI.I (ed. J.C. Rolfe, London and New York, 1927, Vol. III.130–131).

2. In modern times the works of Musonius have been edited by O. Hense, *C. Musonii Rufi Religuiae* (Leipzig, 1903). A later edition with an English translation is that of C.E. Lutz, *Musonius Rufus, "The Roman Socrates"* (New Haven, 1947).

3. Fragment LI (ed. Hense, pp. 132–133).

4. This can be found in *Catonis Reliquiae*, ed. H. Jordan (Leipzig, 1860), *Orationes* V.1., pp. 38–39.

5. In 1893 Dr. W.A. Greenhill published in London a sixth edition of a pamphlet entitled *The Contrast. Duty and Pleasure, Right and Wrong*, in which he gives forty-five quotations on the general theme. The Isocrates quotation is given first (p. 3).

6. Exhortation *To Demonicus*, 45, ed. G. Norlin *Isocrates* (London and New York, 1926), I, pp. 51–52. "For while the result of indolence and love of surfeit is that pain follows on the heels of pleasure, on the other hand, devoted toil in the pursuit of virtue, and self-control in the ordering of one's life always yield delights that are pure and more abiding. In the former case we experience pain following upon pleasure, in the latter we enjoy pleasure after pain."

7. Cicero, in his *De senectute* (XIX.69), however, expresses the same general idea: "Cum enim id evenit, tunc illud quod praeteriit, effluxit; tantum remanet quod virtute et recte factis consecutus sis."

8. *Hieroclis in Aureum Pythagoreorum Carmen Commentarius*, XV (30–31), ed. F.G. Koehler (Stuttgart, 1974), p. 71.

9. Ms B 94. The manuscript is described by W.D. Macray, *Annals of the Bodleian Library, Oxford* (Oxford, 1890), pp. 52–54.

10. *Latin Themes of Mary Stuart, Queen of Scots*, ed. by A. de Montaglon, and printed for the Warton Club (London, 1855).

11. "The Library of Mary Queen of Scots, and of King James the Sixth," in *Miscellany of the Maitland Club* (Edinburgh, 1840) pp. 3–12.

12. The manuscript was first described by G.F. Warner, "The Library of James VI of Scotland," in *The Athenaeum*, Jan. 7, 1893, pp. 16–18. It has been edited by the same scholar in *Miscellany of the Scottish History Society*, I (Edinburgh, 1893), pp. xi–lxxxv.

13. Warner suggests that the quotation must have been provided by one of the tutors of the young king. (*Miscellany*, p. xii).

14. This was reprinted by Richard Hakluyt in 1589 in his *Principal Navigations, Voyages, Traffiques, and Discoveries of the English Nation* (Everyman edition, London and New York, 1937), V,92–120.

15. Sir Humphrey Gilbert, *Discourse of a Discoverie for a New Passage to Cataia* (London, 1576), final page.

16. It is difficult to be dogmatic about this, for the translations are often very free, but the use of the word, "forever", reproducing "semper" in Cato's text, does seem a reliable clue, for it occurs in none of the others.

17. See J.O. Stigall, "The Manuscript Tradition of the *De vita et moribus philosophorum*," *Medievalia et Humanistica* XI (1957), 44–57.

18. Edition of Cologne, ca. 1470, fol. 81^r.

19. "The Church Porch" LXXVII, lines 461–462, *The Works of George Herbert*, ed. F.E. Hutchinson (Oxford, 1953), p. 24. The editor calls attention (p. 483) to Dr. Greenhill's *The Contrast* and notes particularly the use of the proverb by Queen Mary and by Sir Humphrey Gilbert.

20. See F.G. Koehler, *Hieroclis in Aureum*, pp. iii–xxvi.

Notes to Two Renaissance Dialogues

1. See R. Foerster, *Lucian in der Renaissance* (Kiel, 1886) in *Miscellanea Graeca* VI, and F.G. Allison, *Lucian, Satirist and Artist* (Boston, 1926)

pp. 139–150. R.R. Bolgar in *The Classical Heritage and its Beneficiaries* (Cambridge, 1954), pp. 480–481 lists twenty-four Greek manuscripts of Lucian's works that were copied during the fifteenth century. The *editio princeps* of the Greek text was printed by Constantine Lascaris in Florence 1494–1496.

2. See J.E. Sandys, *A History of Classical Scholarship* (New York and London, 1967), II. pp. 36–37.

3. The first manuscript containing three dialogues of Lucian was brought from Constantinople in 1415 by Rinucci da Castiglione. See Bolgar, *The Classical Heritage*, p. 480.

4. The dialogue was printed in Milan in 1497 in an edition of Lucian's *Vera Historia*. There is a copy in the Beinecke Library.

5. For an account of Vegio, *see* L. Raffaele, *Maffeo Vegio* (Bologna, 1909), and A.C. Brinton, *Maphaeus Vegius and his Thirteenth Book of the Aeneid* (Stanford University, 1930), pp. 5–14. The author lists fifty-four treatises written by Vegio (pp. 145–146).

6. See Raffaele, *Maffeo Vegio*, p. 83.

7. There is a copy of this edition in the Beinecke Library. The dialogue is bound with Vegio's *De educatione liberorum*.

8. See Bolgar, *The Classical Heritage*, p. 441 and Allinson, *Lucian, Satirist and Artist*, pp. 147–148.

9. The *Tractatus* was edited by J. Cugnoni, "Aeneae Silvii Piccolomini Opera inedita," in *Atti della R. Accademia dei Lincei* CCLXXX (1882–1883), Third series, pp. 550–615.

10. Ibid., p. 559.

Notes to Some Medieval Impressions of the Ostrich

1. Oliver Herford, *The Platypus*.

2. Ms. II.4.20. A facsimile edition of the manuscript was made by M.R. James for the Roxburghe Club in 1928. In 1954 a translation was made by T.H. White, entitled *The Book of Beasts: Being a Translation from the Latin of the Twelfth Century*.

3. Ms. 189. Another manuscript, 13, of the fourteenth century, has the text without drawings.

4. Yale Marston MS. 80, copied in Italy in 1410, has excerpts from the *Dialogus*.

5. Edited by J.G.Th. Grässe in "Die beiden ältesten lateinischen Fabelbücher des Mittelalters," *Bibliothek des litterarischen Vereins in Stuttgart* CXLVIII (1880) 138–282.

6. Fable 54 (Grässe, pp. 196–197).

7. *P.L.* 177.35–36.

8. *Aurora*, ed. P.F. Beichner (Notre Dame, 1965) I.73, lines 667–672.

9. *De struthione et gallina* and *De struthione et corvo*, ed. J.G.Th. Grässe, "Die beiden ältesten lateinischen Fabelbücher", 39–40, 59. Marston MS. 134 has this text.

10. Ed. T.H. White, pp. 121–122.

11. P. 121.

12. Ed. J. Hastlewood, p. cxv.

13. *Speculum naturale* caps. CXXXVIII–CLX.

14. The badge engraved on the robe of her effigy in Westminster Abbey is reproduced in G.V. Rothery, *Heraldry of Shakespeare* (London, 1930) p. 41.

15. Edition printed in Basel, 1550, p. 1150.

16. Reproduced in G.L. Remnant, *A Catalogue of Misericords in Great Britain* (Oxford, 1969) Plate 11d.

17. *Pseudodoxia Epidemica*, Book II, chapter 22 (*The Works of Sir Thomas Browne*, ed. G. Keynes [Chicago, 1964] II,234–235).

18. Reproduced in A. Henkel and A. Schöne, *Emblemata: Handbuch zur Sinnbild Kunst des XVI–XVII Jahr.* (Stuttgart, 1967) p. 806.

19. Reproduced in J. Nickel, "Der Strauss mit dem Hufeisen in Schnabel," *Hessischer Blätter für Volkskunst* 49/50 (1958), pp. 199–201.

Notes to Le Bon Chien Soullart

1. *Cynegetica* VI, Jacques de Brézé, ed. G. Tilander (Lund, 1959), pp. 56–68. The editor uses the spelling Souillard, but I have kept the reading of the Yale manuscript, Soullart.

2. Jacques du Fouilloux in his *La Vénerie*, chapter V, discusses the St. Hubert dogs, which were black, then mentions the exceptional white dog, Soullart.

3. This authoritative fourteenth-century book on hunting, *La Chasse*, has been edited by J. Lavallée (Paris, 1854).

4. Second edition (Poitiers, 1562), pp. 5–7.

5. *Cynegetica* VI, pp. 27–49.

6. Ibid., pp. 63–66.

7. C. Castets, *Les Chiens courants descendants des Chiens blancs du Roy* (Paris, 1923), p. 7.

8. C.F.G.R. Schwerdt, *Hunting Hawking Shooting* (London, 1928), II, p. 347.

Notes to The American Unicorn

1. *Peregrinatio in Terram Sanctam* (Mainz, 1486). The unicorn is pictured on a page of engravings of the native animals.

2. *Icones animalium* (Zürich, 1560), pp. 62–64, reprinted from the *Bibliotheca universalis* (1551).

3. *Historie of Foure-footed Beastes* (London, 1607), pp. 711–721.

4. *The Principal Navigations, Voyages, Traffiques and Discoveries of the English Nation* (New York, 1937), Everyman's Library ed., VII, 49.

5. Ibid., V, 312.

6. See G.M. Asher, *A Bibliographical and Historical Essay on the Books and Pamphlets Relating to New Netherland* (Amsterdam, 1854–1861), No. 15, p. 23.

7. *The Documentary History of the State of New-York*, ed. E.B. O'Calligan, Vol. IV (1851), Sect. VI, "Description of New Netherland," pp. 113–132. The passage quoted is on page 119.

8. Ibid., p. 120.

9. The unicorn appears again in the right upper corner of a large map of Virginia (p. 134), along with an animal resembling a llama, and a goat.

10. *The Documentary History of the State of New-York*, IV, 1–5, "Great Seals of New Netherland and New-York."

Notes to Abiel Holmes' Life of Ezra Stiles

1. F.B. Dexter, *The Literary Diary of Ezra Stiles, D.D., LL.D.* (New York, 1901).

2. Printed by Thomas and Andrews, Boston, May 1798.

3. Published in New Haven, 1962.

4. Although the book is considered rare, there are a considerable number of copies in American libraries. It has an engraving of Stiles by S. Hill, Boston, opposite the title page.

5. II.429, 452, 527, 542, 568; III.14, 52, 71, 85, 92.

6. *Diary* II.518.

7. III.186–189.

8. III.401.

9. I.476; III.399–400.

10. The portrait is now in the Yale University Art Gallery. It is fully described by Stiles in his *Diary* I.131–133.

11. See *Diary* III.20, 72, 330, 402. A news story in the *New Haven Register* for 13 August, 1978 by Dr. Manuel L. DeSilva reviews the history of the various theories of its origin and concludes that the inscription is Portuguese.

12. Holmes recounts at length the episode of the theft of President Clapp's manuscripts and likens the loss of the valuable documents to the destruction of the famous library at Alexandria (263–264).

13. *Lives by Izaak Walton*, ed. G. Saintsbury (Oxford, 1927), p. 319.

Notes to *A Family Tablet*

1. Abiel Homes, *The Life of Ezra Stiles, D.D., LL.D* (Boston, 1798), pp. 296–301.

2. *The Literary Diary of Ezra Stiles, D.D., LL.D.* ed. F.B. Dexter (New York 1901), III.32. The Valedictory Oration, in Latin, with Honeywood's sketches of Dr. Stiles and himself, is preserved in the Beinecke Library.

3. *Life*, p. 301. In his *Diary* (III.240–244), Stiles records the journey from September 20 to October 23, 1786, and mentions Honeywood several times but he does not relate the incident given in Honeywood's letter.

4. *Poems of St. John Honeywood, M.A.* (New York 1801), p. 5. I follow the preface for the facts of Honeywood's life.

5. Ibid., p. 12. About this same journey Stiles records a very interesting episode (*Diary* III.241–242). He says, "Mr. Honeywood took the Picture of the Grasshopper, Sachem of the Oneida Nation; who solemnly and publicly adopted Mr. Honeywood into the Oneida and Tuscarora Nations by the Name Yohowaunha—a great Rode—by which Indians might travel into Immortality, by Painting."

6. This leaf was apparently torn from the *Diary*, but it was given to the Yale Library by Lewis Stiles Gannett in 1958. In the center of the page President and Mrs. Stiles are drawn in large oval frames, facing each other; above, in three smaller ovals, are portraits, also in profile, of Kezia Taylor, Ezra, Jr., and Elizabeth; below the parents' portraits, also in three ovals, are portraits of Ruth, Isaac, and Emilia; in a smaller oval at the bottom is the portrait of Mary. It is signed "S.J. Honeywood pinxit Jan. 9, 1781."

7. *A Family Tablet*, Preface.

8. In the preface to his edition of the poems, Holmes says that he included some poems foreign to the general design in order to complete the volume. This would explain the inclusion of the "Yaratildia" poem.

9. As to the subsequent history of St. John Honeywood, several years after his departure from New Haven, when he was practicing law in Salem, he married the daughter of Colonel Mosely of Wakefield and had a number of happy years before his early death in 1798. He left a record of his change of fortune in a light-hearted poem "The Sweets of Matrimony Triumphant, or One Bachelor Converted" (*Poems* pp. 53–56). In it he recalls that as a "love-crost Bard," with all hopes disappointed, he whined and, like the fox in the fable, declared that the grapes were sour, or he wrote rueful songs and barbed poems. Then one day Pegasus playfully threw him and, as it chanced, Hymen raised him up and promised to bind him with his magic chain. Now he lives happily married, "in joyful bondage free," and he encourages other swains to follow his example.

Notes to Colonel David Humphreys

1. *The Literary Diary of Ezra Stiles, D.D., LL.D.*, edited by F.B. Dexter (New York, 1901) II.571.

2. This unusual friendship is noted in the last line of an epitaph composed by John Trumbull—"Here Humphreys rests—belov'd of Washington." Humphreys is buried in the Grove Street Cemetery in New Haven. The Latin inscription on his tombstone was written by Benjamin Silliman of Yale. See *Life and Times of David Humphreys* by F.L. Humphreys (New York, 1917), II.436–441.

3. The name is given as Humphrey or Humphreys in Stiles' *Diary* and in other contemporary records.

4. Entitled "Colonel David Humphreys Presenting to Congress the Colors Captured at Yorktown," it was painted by an unidentified artist, possibly a Spaniard. See *Life and Times*, I.235–237.

5. Humphreys' letter is printed in *Life and Times*, II.135–137.

6. This daughter had been baptized Emilia, but at this time she was often called Amelia, as she signs herself on the flyleaf of a book, also from the Foote library, "Amelia Stiles Book, 1790."

7. A facsimile reproduction of this edition, with an introduction by W.K. Bottorff, was published by Scholars' Facsimiles & Reprints, Gainesville, Florida, in 1968.

8. *Life and Times*, I.328, 342; II.316–317.

9. P. 116.

10. *Life and Times*, I.144.

11. Quoted in *Life and Times*, I.146.

Note: Though David Humphreys is now often called General Humphreys, I have referred to him as "Colonel", the term he himself used. The rank of Brigadier-General of the Veteran Volunteers was given him in 1813.

Index